A Sailor
Came To
Newport

Autobiographical
Narrative

Edward T Duranty

This book is dedicated to my very good friend Ted Michaud.

While serving in the Republic of Vietnam as a Marine Engineer, he stepped on a concealed enemy land mine. He suffered multiple shrapnel wounds and a severed leg. (A Newport Marine}

Semper fi

INTRODUCTION

I represent just one of the thousands of sailors that made Newport, Rhode Island, their Port of Call.

Navy men and women began receiving orders to Newport, as far back as 1883. Over time, they raised families, purchased necessities, paid debts, managed sickness, enrolled in schools, attended churches, found employment, all while enduring long separations from their loved ones.

In turn, the people of Newport extended their hand in a gesture of welcome. Bonds of lasting friendships were established between sailors and civilians. Newport was a navy town.

Sailors, coming to Newport, brought with them storied narrations of their pre-navy days. These sagas, where used in a never-ending dialog, to promote and enhance individually, over fellow white hats. More often then not, these tales of grandness were used in the pursuit, of a young ladies companionship.

"Possibly, a Fall River girl!"

.   I arrived in Newport, in August, of 1958. To the best of my knowledge, the writings contained in this book are somewhat factual, well sort of! After fifty odd years of imbibing various liquid refreshments, the memory genes become squishy. I definitely tend to exaggerate, especially if it's a figment of my imagination, or a right out lie.

True facts are not possible, being that as a young sailor in Newport, I lost several million-brain cells, in Jim Shay's Tavern.

The introduction of this book dwells on my pre-navy life. Every sailor is a unique individual that relates his personal life experiences, in the form of a sea story. You can always tell, if it's going to be a sea story. They all begin with:

"This is no shit!"

I would be negligent if I didn't give an example. Joe Milner, (A Sailor Came to Newport) served aboard the Submarine Aspro, during WWII. He swore that this was no shit.

"The Sub was moored to the pier, when Betty Hutton, came aboard for a visit. All went well, but when she left, she had to climb the ladder, to the conning tower. She looked down, to a multitude of heads, all facing upwards. She exclaimed! "You better take a good look; it will be some time before you see it again. Years went by and Betty Hutton was found as a housekeeper, at the St. Anthony's Parish, in Portsmouth, RI. Finding this out, Joe called her up and explained who he was and when she visited the sub. The first thing she said.

"Your not one of those sailors that were looking up my dress were you?"

My Sea Story

"This is no shit!"

I was born, raised, and attended school in Whitefield, New Hampshire. Whitefield is a typical, small New England drinking town, with a hunting problem. An average population, of two thousand hearty souls, it is nestled in the heart of the White Mountains. It lies in the shadows of Mt. Washington, the highest peak in the Northeastern, United States.

The township is well known for it's heavy accumulations, of winter snow. It's resident's, having the fortitude to endure the harsh cold, thoroughly enjoy every minute of it.

In 1956, I graduated from Whitefield High School. There were two classmates; that would be starting college, at the University of New Hampshire. Having influential parents, three of my classmates, walked into good company jobs. The possibilities locally were the Gilman paper Mill or logging for the Brown Company, in nearby Berlin. You could try for a State Highway position or maybe work at a local Post Office. They both had the same response.

"Sorry no openings."

A not so popular alternative would be to heed, the calling of the church and become a nun or a priest. A few of the class jocks were looking, into joining the Marines. A few of us were still wandering around in the dark, continually looking, for that pot of gold, at the end of the rainbow.

Whitefield was one beauty of a place to grow up in. No television, no interstate highways, along with unbelievable fishing and deer hunting. Our seclusion from the rest of the world brought forth the ultimate joy, of living in a pure, clean, environment.

With the addition of a new snowfall, and the gleaming light, from a full moon, schoolmates would meet, pick out a hill, and ski the night away. Fatigued, wet, and cold, we would end up dragging our soggy snow covered bodies home.

Winters in Whitefield, could be extremely harsh. It was worse, when I had to cross over the back yard, snow up to my ass, and shovel my way, to the outhouse!

It was, a really bad place in the summer. A multitude of flies would greet you at the door. Plus, there was no escaping the smell of decaying human waste, rising upward from the pit. A true benefit was the immediate clearing of my sinus congestion.

In the winter, it became an entirely different ball game. Our house had a wood burning stove in the living room. It gave off heat, but always burned out during the night.

On real cold nights, when the temperature dropped down to thirty or forty below zero; I would sleep with my grandfather. Very little heat from the living room reached the upstairs. My grandfather and I would sink into his feather bed mattress, under piles of blankets and quilts. We wore long legged underwear, heavy woolen socks, and wool knitted ski caps pulled down over our ears.

I hated to see the morning come. The outhouse was located some distance from the back door. I had to recon, my way through three feet of snow, with the thermometer showing nineteen below zero.

Having an outdoor toilette, it was my chore, to collect the chamber pots, from inside the house and dispose of their contents. One at a time, I would make my way across the frozen tundra, to the sewage disposal site.

Once, I shoveled the snow a way from the door; I was able to step inside. Brushing the snow off my boots, I would feel the warmth of being sheltered, from the outside cold.

I would have to make, two or three trips, back and forth, leaving the pots lined up on the floor. When I had them all collected, I would shut my eyes, and empty each one down an open seat hole.

Like frozen popsicles, the gobs of feces slid out of the pots. I listened for the sound of impact, when they landed, on the frozen pile below.

That task completed, I would return to the kitchen, and prime our cast iron pump. Lifting the handle up and down, while pouring water into the top orifice, would start an internal suction. Acting like a siphon, it would draw up the water, from deep underground. Filling a bucket full of water, I would return to the outside snow banks, to wash out the chamber pots.

We did not lack for cold water. I washed up from a pan of water warmed up on the kitchen stove. Cleaned and dressed, I was ready for school. My mother would see to it that I had a good breakfast, check my clothing and send me on my way.

The school was over a mile away, but not far enough to rate riding on a school bus. I can never remember, ever having a day off from school, due to the cold, wind, or snow.

Arriving at school, everyone's outer clothes and boots would be matted with frozen snow and ice. The teacher would have us place our outer clothing, in piles in the back of the room so that they might thaw out.

The cold blistering wind, against the face, caused copious amounts of snot, to drain from the nose. It would freeze solidly, against the face and stick to the sides of our mittens. I had never thought about it, but I would guess that's where the term, "snot face," originated.

My girlfriend, who one day would become my wife, lived several miles away in Dalton. Their town's school only went to the sixth grade.

Seventh grade on were transported to the Whitefield School by bus. If it happens to be snowing and the bus got stuck, then the riders would empty out and start pushing.

You're asking what does this have to do with **A Sailor Came to Newport**? Very little but were on the path to Newport.

Thousands upon thousands of sailors left their footprints on the walkways of Newport. Each one was an individual, and each one came from somewhere. Each one had a life they left behind. I'm relating mine, as a casing point, for all the Sailors that came to Newport.

Whitefield's claim to fame was the home of the Mountain View Hotel. Everyone in town knew that the owner was Frank Dodge. I didn't know Frank personally. Being employed as a caddy and window washer, we never crossed paths. Sometime during my association with the Mountain View Hotel, he retired and left the hotel to his son, Schuyler.

Schuyler was running the place during my tenure. He had a gorgeous wife, who played golf every day. I never got to caddy for her, I think I was too dorky looking.

Employed as a caddy, at the Mountain View, I became aware, of what I believed was, a disguised discrimination policy. It may have included other North Country hotels, but I would have no way of knowing. The employees of the hotel, as well as the local towns people, were well aware that Jews were not welcomed at the Mt. View.

I was young and in my teens, but I came to realize that Jews didn't check into the Mountain View. The policy was nonchalantly accepted. The citizens of Whitefield were well aware of Frank Dodges policy.

As I became older, I wondered if "no Jews," was against the law? When I inquired around town, the answer was always.

"He owns the hotel; he can do what he wants."

The Mount Washington Hotel located at the base of Mt. Washington, was approximately twenty-five miles from the Mountain View. We were fifteen miles away from the Maplewood Hotel, in Bethlehem and around ten miles, to the Waumbek Country Club, in Jefferson.

The area hotels would sponsor inter-hotel golf tournaments. Here's the rub to this story. It didn't matter, the religious denomination, of a guy hitting off the first tee.

If the tournament was at the Maplewood, fact was, I wouldn't be there, nor any of my fellow Mt. View caddy's. I could not caddy at the Mt. Washington hotel, or the Bethlehem hotels. I was not Jewish. The Jewish caddy's at the Mt. Washington Hotel, could not caddy at the Mountain View, they were Jewish.

Was this ever documented? I don't know; I wouldn't think so. Most people, In Whitefield had no clue what so ever to Mr. Dodge's viewpoints.

During the summer months, the Mountain View Hotel, provided for one of the largest payrolls, in the North Country. The people of Whitefield were not about to rock the boat, by expounding on Mr. Dodge's philosophy. Jew's inquiring at the Mr. View, were directed to the Spaulding Inn, a little over a mile down the road. Fact or fiction, I couldn't say.

The town of Bethlehem was located fifteen miles south of Whitefield. A welcome sign, on the outskirts of Bethlehem, boasted of having thirty separate hotels. Nearly all were wooden structures, old, and built in a hodgepodge, of sizes and shapes.

When the morning temperatures began to cool down, it signaled that fall was on its way. Guests began an exodus back to the cities. Owners ensured that windows were boarded up, and water pipes drained. All safeguards necessary, to protect their properties, against the onslaught of a cruel winter, were put in place.

With the coming of spring, the process would reverse. While the hotels prepared to reopen, the township braced themselves for the return of the flock, and all the hustle and bustle that went with a new summer.

My grandparents lived several miles from Bethlehem, on the Ammonoosuc River. Each summer, I would spend two weeks living with them. On our first trip to Bethlehem, I remember being amazed to see so many people. They were sitting on hotel porches, street benches, crowding their way in and out store fronts, while other groups, were strolling along both sides, of the main thoroughfare.

I asked my grandparents where did so many people come from? My grandmother was quick to answer.

"There Jews, all of them. They come for the summer then leave. So many of them we have to go to Littleton to shop."

By the tone of her voice, I decided not to inquire further.

Arriving from the city, they came in large numbers, to enjoy the summer months, nestled in the serenity, of the White Mountains. There were families, groups, seniors and teenagers. The afore mentioned, came in droves, with high hopes of finding a summer job

Caddies seldom traveled to other hotels, involving golf tournaments. The host hotel would assign a caddy to each guest. There was an exception, when the tournament was played, at the Waumbec Country Club in Jefferson. I was one of the caddies, selected to accompany the Mountain View golf team. As far as I could determine, there was not, a Jewish caddy on the premises, and I'm not too sure about a Jewish team. No matter where the tournaments were held, the hotel and players were never designated or wore any t name identification.

Why the fixation on this issue? Good question. My peers expounded on the perils of disaster.

"If the Jews were ever to take control of our banking systems, they would buy us out, and we would loose everything."

Such discussions were full of inconsistencies, contradictions and fabricated information. It gave the town folks, some thing to gossip about.

Though this whole period of my life, caddy or no caddy, I had no idea what a Jew was! I could never pick one out; because nobody ever told me, what he or she Jew, was suppose to look like!

I got a few of my buddies together.

"Billy, what's a Jew?"

He thought for a few minutes.

"Jew's can't eat pork if they do they become one of us!"

I turned to Gene.

"Gene, do you go along with that?"

He slowly contemplated his reply.

"I heard talk about the pork thing, but I don't know anything about it. Last week I was in the woods with my father, and I asked him.

"What's a Jew, Dad? Is there a way you can tell a Jew?"

We sat down on a log; he put his hand on my shoulder.

"Son, all know about Jews, is that they don't go hunting."

My Dad's answer caught me by surprise; I had no recourse but to ask why?

"They can't waste the time son; they have to spend it on getting rich."

Gene was not much help, all I knew so far was that Jews didn't go hunting, and they didn't eat pork.

I asked the same question to my best friend.

"Danny, being a Catholic, what's a Jew?"

Before answering, Danny made the sign of the cross. He was protected!

"Last week after mass, I asked that very question, of my parish Priest. I explained that half the town was jawing about Jews and none of us knew what a Jew was."

Billy and Gene moved in closer. They wanted to hear what the priest had told Danny.

"He didn't say too much. He kept referring to me as, "my son."

Holding out his prayer book, he opened it and held it, so I could see pages.

"The answer is in here. People, who don't believe in Jesus are Jews."

His answer was confusing. Remembering my catechism, I fired back.

"Jesus was the Son of God, do Jews believe he was illegitimate?"

The priest, looked up into the sky, like he was looking for inspiration. Closing his prayer book he turned to walk away.

"Danny, I have a funeral to tend to. We will have to go over this some other time."

Are you a Jew or a non-Jew, in the North Country it really doesn't matter, that era has passed by. At the Mountain View Hotel, caddies have been replaced with electric golf carts. Discrimination no longer exists, with the exception of few WWII Veterans, who refuse to ride, in a Jap made golf cart.

"Keep the golf stories going."

On June 24, 1955, President Dwight

Eisenhower visited Whitefield to play golf, at the Mountain View Hotel. The Mountain View Hotel was a favorite of the President. The owner of the hotel had converted a room into a library and dedicated it to President Eisenhower. The library has a display of photos, and memorabilia, from his visits to the hotel.

The Caddy Master assigned me to caddy, for the President's Press Secretary. I had no idea who he was, but was quickly informed that his name was James Hagerty.

A small crowd gathered on the first tee, as the President's foursome were getting ready to tee off. Sherman Adams was in the Presidents group, along with the hotel's golf pro, Frank Brunel and the forth being a Mr. Baker, who I really didn't know.

I presented a golf card to the President, and he autographed it. Years later, while serving on the USS Albany. His grandson, David Eisenhower, added his signature to the same card.

I was disappointed that I didn't get to caddy in the Presidents foursome. However, I would be following the president as Mr. Hagerty, was next off the tee.

The president teed up and swung. His ball sliced, trailing well off into the woods. To my knowledge, no one ever owned up to finding his ball.

Mr. Hagerty made a good tee shot; it passed the two hundred yard marker.

Two other gentlemen joined Mr. Hagerty, making it a threesome. I'm not sure, but Mr. Hagerty's actions seem to indicate that they were members of the Press Corps. Their caddies were my friends. We gave each other the high sign, grabbed their golf bags and trudged off toward the first hole.

I was quite surprised, when Mr. Hagerty approached me, to explain the joining of the other two men. If you were ever a caddy, you know what it's like, never be spoken to.

With people staged all over the fairway, play was very slow. I assumed; the people along the tree line were Secret Service Agents and the New Hampshire State Police. A man walking a few feet behind us was carrying a portable phone. I was sure that it was for Mr. Hagerty's use.

Not only did Mr. Hagerty turn out to be a man of extreme importance, he turned out to be one hell of a nice guy. While we waited for the foursome in front of us, he brought up several questions, on how I was doing in school, and what I wanted to do with my life. He wore a New York Yankee baseball cap and kept ribbing me about the Boston Red Sox.

The President's foursome had cleared the first green and was slowly approaching the second. We had no choice but to stand on the fairway and wait.

To the left of the fairway was a wooded area. It separated the first and second fairways, and concealed the back of the clubhouse. Mr. Hagerty had his attention focused on the tree line.

"Would there be a way through those trees, that would lead us back, to the club house?"

The question seemed a little odd, but I nodded affirmatively.

"I'm not going to follow the old man for the rest of the afternoon."

He gave me a laughing smile.

"Don't tell him I said that, I'll be looking for another job!"

I grinned and hoisted his golf bag to my shoulder.

"I'll tell the other two that I have been called away, then you can blaze a trail through the forest and lead me to the cocktail lounge."

Although disappointed, I did as he requested. We followed the path through the woods, emerging at the rear of the clubhouse. I pointed out the door, which would take him upstairs to the lounge. Asking me to take care of his clubs, he reached to shake my hand. Gripping it tightly, he emphasized that if I ever saw him again, I was to say hello. With that, he slipped me a ten-dollar bill.

I was in deep trouble. Prior to the Presidents arrival, the hotel staff had briefed us. "Anyone taking a tip or any payment from a member of the Presidential party, would be fired immediately and banned from the hotel property."

I had no way out but to tell Mr. Hagerty that I had to refuse his tip, if the hotel knew, I accepted it, I would be fired.

He chuckled and put the ten in my shirt pocket.

"I'm not going to tell anyone, are you?"

I thought that over. I met the Presidents Press Secretary, went two holes, and pocketed a ten-dollar tip. Not bad, not bad at all!"

I graduated from Whitefield High School and through the support of my family and relatives; I was accepted to attend Plymouth Teachers College, located in Plymouth, N.H.

I don't want to drag this segment out as it is not one of my prouder moments. The college had a continent of Korean Veterans, attending college, under the GI Bill. They were a rough lot, drinking and raising hell. At eighteen, it was easy to be intimidated.

The President of the college suspended me for one semester for miss-conduct. Upon my return, I would be placed on academic probation. When I called home with the news, the reaction was disastrous and sad. This is where I showed my maturity!

"Screw the President and his college, I'll join the Navy."

I reported for Boot Camp, in January, of 1958. I thought back in New Hampshire that at twenty below zero, it just couldn't get any colder. I was wrong!

At the Great Lakes Naval Training Center, a wind chill factor, at zero temperatures was far worse. Moist, frigid, air rising up from the surface of Lake Michigan blew in strong gusts, straight across the training center. The wind was wet, bone-chilling and freezing. No matter how you dressed, the cold wet chill penetrated into every part of your body. It was most enjoyable, when you were out on the parade field, learning how to march!

There were eight or nine Blacks in my company. Until boot camp, I had never met a Black person. During the summer back home, I would spot an occasional, Black chauffeur driving through town.

The first few weeks our training dealt with being transformed into sailors. We were getting to know each other, and although friendships were beginning to form, there was discourse among us.

It was apparent to me that some of the whites, especially those from the south, would continually talk down to a Black. The Blacks, in turn, stayed together in a click. You would never see one of them alone.   Animosity toward each other took place on a daily basis. Those in charge ignored it.

Contemptuous smiles, smirks, jeers and insulting remarks, were used openly between the two factions. This behavior was identical to what I had witnessed back home between the locals and the Jews. I tried to comprehend the reasoning behind their actions. I just wasn't experienced or educated enough, to understand the ingrained and deep-roots of their prejudices. In a time, I would. Hell, I was still trying to find out what a Jew was!

Chapter 1

While home on Boot Camp leave, I popped the question and became engaged. I gave her a diamond ring that she still wears to this day. I purchased it at the Base Exchange, Great Lakes, Illinois, for the sum of sixty-five dollars.

After I had completed Boot Camp, I received orders for Hospital Corps School. It was ironic, as it was located across the street from Boot Camp. Upon completion of Corps School, and in possession of an approved

"Special Request Chit" from the Navy, during my leave we were married.

I had received; my first set of orders, for the U.S. Naval Hospital, Newport, RI,

Because of the uncertainty of housing, transportation, and what my duties would be, we decided it best that I report to my first duty station alone. The plan was that she would live with her parents until I could find an apartment.

Chapter 2

Towing my sea bag behind me, I got off the Short Line Bus, in front of the Navy YMCA, in downtown Newport, Rhode Island. (**A Sailor Came to Newport**)

The first thing catching my eye were that there were Sailors everywhere. A large group were milling around the front of the YMCA building, they were taking up most of the front steps.

Standing beside my sea bag, I was trying to decide on what to do, but most of my time was being spent saluting Officers. I was getting a few stares, and a whole lot of grins, from the crowd on the steps. A sea bag and two little white stripes, it wasn't too hard to figure out, "Boot Camp!"

One of the sailors standing on the upper step caught my attention.

"Hey Boot! You don't have to salute them assholes; they're Officers Candidates. Nothing but a bunch of fucking college pukes!"

I had no idea who Officers Candidates were, but I accepted the advice and cut short the saluting. The grinning ceased and I got my first ear full, of how sailors express themselves.

A Cozy cab drove up and stopped at the curbside. The driver got out and approached me on the sidewalk.

"Where you headed Admiral?"

Again, I heard laugher from the front steps crowd. Having no idea where I was or what to do, I decided to go with the cabbie. It would be better, then spending the rest of the day, standing on the sidewalk, holding up my sea bag

"I have orders, to report for duty at the Newport Naval Hospital."

Grabbing the strap on my sea bag, he pointed to the sailors, standing on the steps.

"You can check with anyone of those swabbies and they will tell you, the bus does not go to the Naval Hospital. There is one bus; that will let you off on Connell Highway, but your still left with a good walk, especially carrying a sea bag.

He did mention that the hospital would send a car; if I told them I was a Captain.

23

"The best way mate, is to put your self and your sea bag in the cab and leave the driving up to me."

Not having a lot of choices, I agreed. Taking a seat in the back of the cab, I was convinced that I made the right decision. All in all, the cabbie seemed to be a pretty nice guy.

He started making conversation the minute we left.

"All these old streets are constantly under repair and one-way. They have it set up, so you have to go down First Street, up Second Street and down Third Street, which is fairly close to the hospital. To get to it, I have to cross over on to Farewell Street, past Van Zandt Avenue and onto Connell Highway. That's where I mentioned the bus stops. From Connell Highway, we cross over a set of railway tracks, then take a sharp left."

The Cabbie continued to talk and keep my attention, by pointing to the rear of the hospital buildings.

"Here we go mate, a sharp turn, and then a hard right, and you have arrived at the Naval Hospital."

I was so intrigued at scoping out the hospital and the ocean view that I didn't notice there was no construction, on Third Street.

"The hospital, has the only gate where there are no guards. All the gates on the main base have Marine Sentries."

We pulled under an archway and came to a stop.

"This is where you check in, the main desk is just inside."

When I got out of the cab, he was standing with my sea bag, positioned in front of the main entrance.

"The meter reads twenty-one dollars; that's without a tip. Twenty-five would square us away."

It was way more than I could afford, and it ate deep into my funds. In 1958, that was one hell of a fare. At that moment, I wish I had walked.

Being a young sailor in Newport, it was easy for the cabbie to take me for a ride! Looking back, I remembered his grooming and dress. He could have been in the Navy and moonlighting a second job. It was a sad thought that he would make his living, leeching off his fellow sailors. I would soon learn that the practice was fairly prevalent.

Checking in for duty was a quick process. Once I was logged in, the Chief on duty gave me directions to the corpsmen's quarters. It was located at the far end of the compound. I was dragging my sea bag when I finely got there.

My new home, was a large brick building, housing four separate dormitories, on two levels. Each had approximately thirty bunk beds. I was assigned to the dorm, on the ocean side, second floor. My bunk was in the back and of course I was given the top rack.

Next to my rack was a steel locker to stow my gear in. I was informed never to leave my locker unguarded, unless it was padlocked. I had been smart enough to bring a lock with me, but it made me nervous that a fellow corpsman would rip me off.

The sailor in charge of the dorm was a First Class Petty Officer and a lifer. (A Sailor Came to Newport) The four hash marks on his sleeve, told me he was nearing twenty years of service or longer. He noticed my frown.

"I've been in the Navy for a long time, I'm not a Corpsman, I am a Machinist Mate. I have spent most of my time riding destroyers. This billet is considered to be my shore duty. With all that said, I do know one thing to be true. Many sailors are not, who you think they are. Take everything in stride, and keep a sharp watch on yourself. You're in the best Navy in the world, but never forget, there are always a few rotten apples, in every barrel."

It had been a hell of a first day. My gear squared away; I padlocked my locker, made up my bunk then lifted myself to it. Lying on my stomach, I could see out of a small window, at the ocean's shoreline. The barracks was built on the shores of a small cove. High tides and rough seas, washed up against a granite wall, built to protect the compound.

Looking in the opposite direction, I took immediate interest, in a building across the street. It was wood constructed and resembled an old military barracks.

It was encircled, with a ten-foot chain fence, with a row of barbed wire stretched out along the top? From the fence, to the building there were no obstacles, just bare ground.

There was one entrance gate, in the front of the building. I thought it might be used, to house naval prisoners or severe psychotic patients. I fell asleep still guessing.

The next morning, after I had cleaned up, and dressed, I went down to the first floor and peered across the street. I hadn't even guessed close. A large sign, attached to the fence read,

"WAVE'S BARRACKS"

Chapter 3

Several Corpsmen were getting ready to report for their shifts. (A Sailor Came to Newport) They gave me a fast welcome aboard and let me know that the galley was in the hospital's main building. I had twenty minutes to make breakfast. I wasted no time, getting my young ass there. After one hell of a meal with eggs and bacon, I reported to the personal office.

Handing my records to the Chief, he gave them a quick scan, then tossed them, on a pile of records, on his desk. (A Sailor Came to Newport) The Chief wasted little time. I got the welcome aboard spiel, at the same time, he was handing me my check-in-sheet.

"If you can't find some of these places, just ask. When you're finished, bring the list back to me. Words of warning Doc don't be screwing around on my time. I'm no one to fuck with."

I promptly assured him, I would do what I was told, and would return post haste.

"Look sailor, first thing is you call me my first name, "Chief." The second thing is nobody gives a shit, if you goof off or not. You do what you have to do, any goddamn way you want. If you're caught goofing off, and it comes back on me. I will say; I told him not to fuck around. I'm covered; it's your ass that's going to hang. The moral of this spiel is, I can do no wrong, I walk on water, got it?"

Shaken, I answered sharply.

"I got it Chief."

Making an about face, I doubled time it out of there. When I returned I got my first break, the Chief was gone. A second class had my records, and with a twist of his wrist, motioned me to take a seat. (A Sailor Came to Newport)

"The Chief left your checking in to me. He has these important meetings at the CPO Club that mandate his presence."

He snickered and held back the urge to laugh.

"The CPO Club is right outside gate four, know where it is?"

I shook my head.

"Us low life bastards can't go in, but from what I hear, the place is full of chicks from Fall River, all wanting just one thing."

I wasn't sure just what in the hell he was talking about and let it slide.

"Okay, you're being assigned to Ward E, it's an orthopedic ward, broken bones and all that crap. Don't frown; the Chief could have put you in the pediatric ward changing shitty diapers all day. He's saving that detail for the first ass hole that mouths off to him.

Big smile on his face, he handed me my assignment sheet.

"Go topside to the first floor and check in with Commander Martin. She is the head nurse, and her office is just past the main desk. Don't be falling in love!"

Standing, he reached out and shook my hand.

"Welcome aboard, if there is anything I can ever do for you, just let me know."

I gave him a quick tip of my hat and headed for the stairwell.

Chapter 4

Commander Martin scared me. Standing at attention in front of her desk, she merely glanced up while she was flipping through my service jacket. She minced no words, and gave me a five-minute lecture on what she expected from her corpsmen. There would be no warnings; she didn't believe in giving any. What the alternative was, she didn't say. Her starch, white nurse's uniform coordinated nicely, with her gold braided nurses cap. It did nothing to compliment the appearance, of one mean looking old lady.

"You may call me Miss Martin, when a dire medical emergency exists. Only then, do you have permission to approach me. Your supervising nurse is Miss Lewis. You will direct all your inefficiencies and excuses directly to her. Any questions?"

I had none and told her so.

"Then leave my office, and report to Lt. Lewis on Ward E."

I was dismissed. That would be the first and last time, that Miss Martin ever acknowledged my existence, during my tour of duty at the hospital.

After her retirement, I read in the Daily News that she had passed away in her sleep. Her body lay undiscovered for some time before being found. Sad, where were her friends?

Miss Lewis, turned out to be a peach. With her training, I was able to learn quickly, the duties of working on a ward. Two corpsmen were on duty during the day, one on the evening shift and one on the night shift. I worked days until Miss Lewis, certified that I was competent, in all phases of ward duty, and qualified for the night duty. Shortly after, I was assigned, to the four to eleven shifts.

On my off hours, I spent walking the streets near the hospital, looking for an apartment. As it turned out, luck was with me, and I found a small, vacant, second-floor apartment, at 51 Second Street. It was small, but within walking distance, of the hospital. We had no car or television and not much of anything else, but it would be our first home together.

Chapter 5

The Newport Daily News, dated October 15, 2009, printed a "Then and Now," photograph and history, of 51 Second St.

The article stated that in 1725, Solomon Townsend built a house at 51 Second Street, for his residence. Staying in the family, it was sold in 1770, to Thomas Rodgers. In 1850, it was sold to W. Hamilton Jr. In 1971, Joseph

Silvia, bought the house and two years later, sold it to Newport Restoration Foundation. The house is listed on the National Register of Historic Places.

So what was missing from that article? From 1959 to when ever, I would refer to the Hamilton House as the "Slum Period." The photo will show, that the house was not that big. The before photo, is somewhat like I remembered.

The house had been made into four shabby, separate, furnished apartments. We were on the second floor, when looking at the right side, of the building. There was a sofa, chair, lamp stand, kitchen table and chairs, some utensils, stove, small bathroom and a very small bedroom abutting the neighbor's wall.

The apartment across from us was a bit larger, as their bedroom hung out away from the house, on two wooden stilts. We kidded, that some day the stilts would give away, and they would land on the ground, bed, and all. (A Sailor Came to Newport) We didn't get to know them very well; as shortly after they were transferred to the west coast. We moved into their larger apartment.

Three days later, Mary Lou and her husband moved in to our old apartment. (A Sailor Came to Newport)

Mary Lou was something else. She 'was a blond and very well endowed. Her husband was a Fireman aboard one of the destroyers.

Poor bastard never got home. Mean while Mary Lou, had more overnight guests than the Holiday Inn. The coup de grace, came, when she made it known that she was pregnant, and then asked my wife, if I could bring some medical instruments home to get rid of the baby.

That was our last contact with Mary Lou; her husband came home a few days later, spent less than an hour and went back to his ship. Mary Lou left, stiffing the landlady out of the month's rent.

The dollar amount of the rent escapes me. A white haired, elderly lady promptly came for the rent on the first of each month. I think her name might have been MacFherson. She flipped out at Mary Lou leaving.

The top floor apartment, housed a First Class Boatswain's Mate. (A Sailor Came to Newport) His wife or maybe it was his girl friend was Arleen C. He too was on a destroyer that spent a lot of time at sea. They used to have some lulu fights.

She would be a mess. The minute he went to sea, Arleen was in her glad rags and downtown she went. When Arleen had a few drinks, knowing I was a corpsman, she would ask if I could go up to her apartment to see if she were pregnant.

No luck there, she dropped the pregnant bit and substituted what she thought was a heart attack. I rushed up the stairway and came back down, three steps at a time. She wanted to show me, where her heart had been relocated! Needless to say, the wife placed Arleen "off limits!"

A wonderful family housed the first-floor apartment, by the last name of Morin. He was a First Class Machinist's Mate, stationed on the USS Severn. (A Sailor Came to Newport)

They were a great family having three children. His wife June was a great asset in helping us, to cope with the hardships, of being a Navy family.

You didn't have to shout to be heard between apartments. The walls being paper-thin, allowed us all, to know each other's business. It was crowded, but we all got along.

Chapter 6

Being newly weds our personal belongings were slim. We did our best, to make a home, but on E-2 pay, things were always tight. Having no car, we had to walk. It wasn't long, and we found out, that there was going to be three of us.

When I first reported to the hospital, the liberty was port and- starboard, meaning every other day off. Shortly there after, it went to a three-section liberty, meaning one day on, two nights off.

My duties on Ward E progressed rather well. Lou Upham was the corpsman on Ward F, which was also an orthopedic ward. (A Sailor Came to Newport)

He was a great deal of help in showing me the ropes. We became friends, but Lou was not cut out to be a lifer. Years later I would run across him working retail. I think it was in a Summerville store. I could be wrong. I do know that Lou is still living in Newport and dabbling in real estate. We go way back.

I was doing quite well, as a ward hospital corpsman, when my world fell apart. As the result of a motorcycle accident, a sailor had been admitted to my ward, with fractures to both legs. (A Sailor Came to Newport)

He was lying on his back; his legs immobilized in a Spica cast.

The cast was molded from his waist down, encompassing both legs, to the ankles. There was a molded cross section, which kept the legs apart and in a locked position. So that he could relieve himself, a cut out was made around his private areas. The opening enabled him to use bedside receptacles, to relieve himself.

Night duty on the ward was all in all, pretty routine. After the patients finished up their night meal, I would clear away the trays and begin the process, of giving the bed patient's, sponge baths. It was still early, when the duty nurse entered the ward and began to make her rounds checking on each patient. No doubt it made the patients feel more at ease to have a nurse talk to them. It certainly kept me on my toes.

When she came to the Spica patient, he complained that he was constipated and was starting to get stomach cramps. She patted him on the shoulder, informing him that she would ensure that his discomfort would be taken care of.

Returning to the ward desk, she wrote orders in his chart and conveyed them to me.

"You're to give him a soap suds enema."

I had only worked with this nurse a few times. I made it a point to inform her that I had never administered an enema. Her instructions, I will never forget.

"Go in the medicine room, and take the enema can off the supply shelf. Check the tube, especially the insert. Put a small amount of the soap into the can, no more than half an ounce. Fill the can to the full line, with warm water. Check to make sure, the soap is mixed in well with the water. Put a dab of KY jelly on the insertion tip then gently insert it into the rectum. Hold the can up, at least a foot above the buttocks. The water has to flow easily down the tube. Most important, have a bed pan at the ready!"

Handing me the patient chart, she emphasized, that I document all aspects of the procedure. With that, she murmured some half ass excuse for leaving, saying she was falling behind on her scheduled rounds.

Using my best bedside manner, I informed the patient, I was going to stick a tube up his ass. He was a Third Class Petty Officer, who's name I have long forgotten. We looked at each other. He was nervous, I was nervous. He asked.

"How big is the tube?"

Assuring him that it was no big deal, I crossed the ward and entered the treatment room. I followed the nurse's orders to the letter. All went well from the insertion, to the lifting of the can. Withdrawing the tube, I instructed him to try and hold the solution inside him for three minutes.

In that little time, I had the bedpan in place, clean bed linen, a pan of water, washcloths and several towels, ready to go. It was during the holding period that all hell broke loose.

His screams of pain scared the hell out of me. He didn't let up and was yelling for a doctor. Getting my act together, I called the front desk and reported an emergency. Within minutes the duty medical officer, a nurse and a contingent of followers rushed into to the ward. I signaled the doctor that I needed help. The Doctor came! The Nurse came! The patient went to the Operating Room!

I had used the wrong soap! What I used was a strong, sanitizing and disinfecting agent. The results were catastrophe. The soap being caustic caused severe pain to the tissue lining of the bowels.

Rushed to the Operating Room, the doctors flushed the inside of the rectal cavity with copious amounts of normal saline. It left the tissue reddened, and extremely sensitive. His next few bowel movements would not be fun. It was early in the morning, before he was returned to the ward. Unfortunately, I was not.

The nurse stated unequivocally that she had given me explicit instructions. The soap to be used was plainly labeled and was clearly visible, inside the medicine cabinet. She was nice enough, not to mention; she was the only one with the key and it was locked. She stressed; I had been taught to learn that any item, outside of the medicine cabinet was not to be used for medicinal purposes.

Guess what? I was not allowed to speak. It was my introduction to the code of the Officers Military Justice.

The next morning, I was told to report to Food Service. My ward days were over; I had a new classification.

"Galley Rat."

Chapter 7

There were a few good points about working in the galley. First of all, everyone treats you like you are dirt and a non-hacker. In order to be sent to the galley you must have fucked up big time. No one much cared; it was your problem to deal with. Just push your chow carts and stay the hell away from the rest of us.

I had put in a special request chit, to see Miss Martin. I wanted to take my case directly to her. She refused. Military justice, I loved it.

The duties, consisted of pushing chow carts to the hospital wards, plus wards located away from the main building. They were referred to as the "P" Wards. In order to deliver to these outposts, the chow carts had to be elevated, and then pushed onto the back of a pickup truck.

There were six P-wards. The truck held two chow carts, which equaled three trips to deliver, and three trips to collect. Most of the time it wasn't bad, but lookout when it rained, and the snows of winter arrived. Like a

Postman, we delivered three meals a day, regardless. In between meals, we unloaded supply trucks.

In reality, my being sent to the galley was a blessing. Having to be at the galley by six in the morning and working until six or seven at night, I was taken off watch bills and had every night off. On the weekend the crew split in half, so every other weekend I had the duty, but was still allowed to go home at night.

It took a load off both our shoulders, as I no longer had to wear a pressed white uniform every day. We had been washing my uniforms in the kitchen sink, then hanging them out the window on a make shift clothesline. The uniform in the galley was a Navy dungaree. I could make them last a week or longer.

On my weekend's off, we would fill a couple of pillowcases with dirty clothes, and walk to the Laundromat off Farewell Street. As my wife neared childbirth, I made the trek alone.

When I reported to the Food Service Office, I was introduced to a big, big, Chief. He would have easily weighed in at three hundred big ones. (**A Sailor Came to Newport**)

The introduction was short, and he motioned me to follow him. We made the rounds of the galley, where I met the Dietician and the Food Service Officer. Bellowing out to the food service workers, he introduced me as the new member of the team. Looking at the expressions on most faces I was of the opinion, I was on the same level as rat shit. With the pleasantries, over, the Chief escorted me into the locker room.

The walls were lined with individual lockers as both civilians and navy personnel shared the facilities. There were several empty chairs and butt cans for people taking a break. Motioning me to one of the chairs, I took his lead and sat down. Standing in front of me, he unbuttoned the front of his Chiefs coat.

"Now piss head, you best listen up. You're here because you're a fuckup! I don't give a shit what you did. I'm telling you while you are here; you had best towed the line. If you screw up under my charge, guess what? No report chits, no transfer, and no nothing. I will take care of your indiscretions."

Grabbing the arms on the chair he lifted the chair and me, off the floor.

"Get the idea sailor? Don't be late for work; don't ever be late for work. Keep clean, work hard."

Setting the chair back on the floor, he stood looking at me.

"Get the hell out of here and go meet the rest of your fellow losers. Keep in mind, if you ever make me look bad, it will be the sorriest day of your life."

I believed him

Chapter 8

Our daughter was born at the Naval Hospital. There were no complications and both mother and baby were well. Upon leaving, we were given a layette and a basket overflowing with various products, for use in infant care. We were very thankful.

The clothing gifts were hand made by a hospital's women's group. Made up of volunteers, they bestowed gifts and love, to every new mother. Thanking everyone, we left with our daughter. We were bringing her home to 51 Second Street.

The administrative functions, involving the hospital stay, the maternity program, was a snap compared to the bureaucracy, I went through to get permission to marry. I was thankful that I didn't have to put in a request, for permission to have a baby.

My mother-in-law took absolute control over my daughter. The best I could do was to stand completely out of the way

Fetching my father in law, and myself a couple of cold beers from the kitchen, I was met by a stern look, from the mother-in-law. Returning, I took my seat and commenced relating the story, of my special request chit, to my father-in-law.

"I was two-thirds of the way, through Hospital Corps School, when I had a scheduled progress meeting with my adviser. During the course of our conversations, I mentioned the fact that I was getting married.

The advisor threw up his arms and shook his head.

"Married, when did you get permission for that?"

"I'm eighteen; I don't need permission in New Hampshire."

"You are wearing the uniform of the United States Navy. You took an oath. You swore allegiance to the President. You accept the Navy's food, housing and pay. That makes you property of the United States Navy."

As hard as I tried, I couldn't understand what in hell he was alluding to. My response was to shake my head negatively.

"Well let me tell you the facts of life Sailor. You belong completely lock, stock and barrel, to the United States Navy. You want to get married, you ask permission. If you get turned down, that's it! You don't get married. You go ahead anyway, and the Navy finds out, they will give you the boot, with a Bad Conduct Discharge."

My father-in-law was listening with interest as I finished up my Sea Story,

"The first special request chit, that I ever submitted, was to the Commanding

Officer, of the Hospital Corps School. I requested that the Navy, give me permission to get married. I sent most of my time trying to come up with, what in hell was I going to do, if my request was refused.

After a week of waiting, I was called to the personnel office and told my request had been approved.

My advisor had the last word.

"If the Navy wanted you to have a wife, they would have issued you one."

Taking a swallow of his beer, my father–in-law was amused.

"The Army didn't give a shit, as long as you remembered, your real wife, was your first sergeant!"

When we brought our daughter home from the hospital, my pay grade was E-2. Before tax's, my pay was $85.00 a' month. My wife's parents often came from New Hampshire and provided us, with a great deal of support. When they left to return home, we were in fairly decent shape.

Reporting for work, I met my fellow "galley rats." In no time, we became tight friends. It was a while ago, but I do remember some names. Cunningham was a hot pistol from upstate Maine. (A Sailor Came to Newport) He had some whooping sea stories, about his adventures on the Indian Reservation.

Wheaton was a jokester from an area north of Boston. (A Sailor Came to Newport)

Johnson I think came out of one of the Boston suburbs. (A Sailor Came to Newport)

Then there was Jim McGrath, a songwriter and singer. (A sailor Came to Newport)

We worked hard, and our civilian counter parts treated us with kid gloves. I dislike mentioning just a few names, but without anyone to ask, it's the best I can do. The galley was closed some time ago. John Mercer ran the supply room. He ordered, and we unloaded the trucks. John was always after us to get his cigarettes at the Navy Exchange. It was hard to refuse him, but it was against regulations!

The cooks were Big Al and "Cowboy." The three badass cooks were Pete, Donald and Seamen. After work, they always went somewhere for a cool brew. On occasion, they would bring us up to West Broadway for a few beers. The bar was predominately black, but our ethnic origin was not a primary concern. We would always have a ball, make friends, and watch our three amigo's bring the house down.

Nick was the senior mess man. A retired Navy cook. (A Sailor Came to Newport) He always made sure that we sat and chowed down. For me, it was a blessing. There was no way I could have afforded to eat at the navy

45

exchange cafeteria or order take out from a local shop.

A few years after Nick retired, I drove by the Breakers, on Ochre Point Avenue. In the middle of the street was Nick, in a security uniform, directing traffic. I couldn't stop, but we waved to each other. It was ironic that thirty years later, I would be dressed in the same security uniform, directing traffic, from the same spot, in front of the Breakers.

Stanley was in charge of the conveyer belt. He stood at the end so he could examine each tray before it went into a food cart. Several food service workers were stationed on each side of the belt. The starter was at the far end of the conveyer. He would place a tray with heating elements on the belt. As the tray moved along the workers would laden it with food, place the heating element over the main dish; add a beverage, silverware and packs of various condiments.

At the end of the line, Stanley would give a nod that tray was complete and insert it into an open chow cart. When it was full, it was our turn to rock and roll and deliver the carts to the wards.

Stanley always wore a tall white paper hat, to conceal his baldness. Wheaton would sneak up on him and knock it off his head. Stan would go bonkers and throw a tantrum. The Chief had to step in and say, "no more!"

The gang would often visit our apartment, to toss down a few beers. Most of the time we were broke and drank my home brew. Some times it was almost a week old.

Our greatest memories were when Gentleman Jim would bring his guitar and sing, "Over the Wall Jake," and "Mule Skinner Blues."

The highpoint of my duty, in food service, occurred on a weekend, when I had the duty with, Jim, Cunningham, and Wheaton.

Same weekend, I got a message that I had made E-3, I think it was because of my time in service. My pay jumped to $99.30 a month, before taxes. Cause for celebration!

I'm not sure how the idea came about, but it was brought up, that the bakeshop was empty. The bakers only did their thing during the weekdays. Smart talk between the four of us, surmised that the area behind the ovens would be a perfect site for a still.

For the life of me, I don't know who constructed it, but I would guess, Cunningham. Just by chance Pete and Donald were the weekend cooks. While we were out scouting copper tubing, the cooks were adding their expertise to the project. The result was something to be proud of.

Delivering the meal carts to the wards, we would commandeer all the denatured alcohol we could find. There was no opposition, the last thing a ward corpsman wanted, was trouble with the galley rats.

"Help yourself, it's in the medicine locker."

The emergency room crew was busy eating gee dunks and bull shitting. Easier than grease on a stick, we eased in and confiscated two quarts, from their backup locker.

You cannot drink denatured alcohol. It is colored, made undrinkable and labeled as such. When we distilled it, the results were a clear liquid. With our combined medical knowledge, we all agreed, it was drinkable!

Next came the ice and orange juice. It was drinkable all right, it didn't take long, and everyone was feeling pretty mellow.

This was against Navy Regulations, and we could find ourselves sucking pond water.

The Food Service Office was located off the galley area. Inside the office were two desks, bookcases, personal photos and an Intercom system. The intercom system was wired into the officer's mess and the enlisted dinning room. Very seldom used, its main function was to make emergency announcements.

The office housed the Dietitian and the Food Service Officer. The desk located closest to the entrance door belonged to the Food Service Officer. I can't spell his name, but it was like Fuquay, or Feuquay. He didn't bother us much, but you knew he was always watching. He had advanced from the enlisted ranks, to being a Lieutenant, in the Medical Service Corps. He was known as a Mustang and no one to try and bull shit. (A Sailor Came to Newport)

He had been there, done it. He thought of us as his "boys." The foremost reason why no one fucked with us.

When he was commissioned, he received an ebony pen set, inscribed with his name and the date of his commissioning. It was a symbol of his accomplishment and it sat honorably, at the center of his desk.

Considering the strength of our brew, things were going pretty well on schedule. All the chow carts had been delivered to the wards, which left us an hour before they had to be retrieved.

We were hanging in the Food Service Office. I don't remember, just how it came about, but Jim had taken over the Lieutenants chair. Propping his feet on top of the desk, he began to strum on his guitar. His next move was incredible. Reaching to a small cabinet, he flicked on the power button to the intercom system. The output led to a speaker in the Officers mess and two in the General mess.

49

Strumming a few loud cords for back up he spoke into the systems microphone.

"This is Gentleman Jim,"

I'm not so sure of Jim's exact words, but they were booming out into the Officers Mess.

"Here to entertain you with a few of my favorite tunes."

With that he on his guitar and broke into, "Over the Wall Jake." A niffy little song about a prison break.

Having lunch in the officer's mess at the time was a doctor, who held the rank of Captain. I don't know why, but behind his back, everyone in the hospital referred to him as, "Black Mac." He was known, not to be friendliest sailor in the crowd. (A Sailor Came to Newport)

When he made his appearance in the galley, we all scattered in different directions, but Jim got caught in the middle of "Mule Skinner Blues."

As things settled down, we all found ourselves on report for misconduct. The "still" had gone undiscovered. The next morning the Command Security Officer briefed the Chief on our weekend activities.

When the Chief returned from the briefing, he had us assemble in the Locker room. He stood us in a row, then moved a bench against the entrance door. Taking a position in front of us, he slowly removed his Chiefs coat and carefully placed it on an empty chair. He loosened the knot in his tie and undid the top button of his shirt. Glaring at each one of us, his hand sprung forward locking on to my throat.

"Let me tell you dumb bastards one thing. The Food Service Officer found his honored pen set broke in half. He is not a happy camper. I have to go in and tell the man, just what you little pricks were up to this weekend. I want every detail, and I want the truth."

Letting go of my throat he yelled in my face.

"If you fuck over me, I can assure you I will kick your ass, have you busted to E-1, and all of you will spend thirty days in the Brig."

Pushing me out of the way, he moved down the line.

"Let's start with the biggest looser in the place. Mr. wise ass Cunningham."

Twelve years later I was stationed at the Naval Prison in Portsmouth, N.H. In the enlisted men's club, I ran into the old Chief. He had been retired for some time. He had no idea who I was until I mentioned the still and my stretched neck. Old Chief's live with their memories; it brought tears to his eye's. He was overjoyed, to go back and relive, the "Mule Skinner Blues." I believe his last name

51

was, Peto, Pero, Perro. I have always remembered his first name, "Chief."

On my days off, we would put our daughter in her stroller, and walk her to a small park off First Street. It was a delightful park with a great view of the harbor. When it was high tide, we were treated to watching the youngsters, dive off the First Street Pier into the cold ocean waters.

There were two shopkeepers, who were instrumental in aiding our well being. The principle source of our groceries, we purchased from a small neighborhood Market across the street from our apartment. It was on the corner of Second and Walnut. The last name I can't remember, but his first name was Walter. He and his wife looked out for us. Because we had no transportation, we purchased most of our daily needs from his market. Towards the end of the month, we would be short on money. Walter would give us what we needed, and we would pay him when we could. I'm glad to say that when we left; our tab was paid in full. I don't know how we made it on ninety dollar a month, but Walter and his wife made it a hell of a lot easier.

Thinking back on those days I don't believe as E-2 or E-3 we were entitled to basic housing nor moving allowances. I got comrats, which was compensation for eating off base. If

I ate at the hospital I had to pay. I believe I got around thirty extra dollars a month. I didn't use it to dine at the hospital, but instead we used it to buy formula for the baby.

If you were to turn off Farewell Street onto Popular Street, you might have found where there use to be a drug store that also featured an ice cream parlor. It could have been in the vicinity of Cross Street. No, I think I am wrong, the more I think about it, the drug store might have been on upper Thames Street. If you turned right off Farewell onto Thames Street, the drug store would have been a short ways down on the right hand side.

The gentleman that we dealt with, was rather tall, wore glasses and had a cropped haircut. I always thought of him to be the owner. I do remember that he always wore a white medical type tech-coat. When we brought our daughter home from the hospital to Second Street, the doctor had put her on a formula of Similac. The drug store was within walking distance and fortunately for us, he stocked the formula.

Similac was available and cheaper on the base, but the walk was too far. Cash flow was a problem. Same with trying to go to the Commissary, by the time you paid the cab fare you weren't saving much. I do remember when I was an E-2 and living in MEMQ we were walking distant to the Commissary.

Let me express a few self-thoughts on the Commissary and the Exchange Stores. The time period was when I held the pay grades E 2, E-3, E-4, which are the bottom pay rates of the heap. We lived at Second Street, Lincoln Street, MEMQ, and Mahan St in Tonomy Hill. In the early sixty's the commissary was located just in side of Gate Four. We would pick up a shopping cart from out side the building and enter the commissary. If there were a line than we would fall in behind the last person. Proceeding down the isles on both sides were cases of can goods with their cardboard tops removed.

Signs indicated prices, Pea's twenty cents a can, and eight for a dollar. Corn eight cans for a dollar, etc. Nothing fancy, the whole store operated like a warehouse operation, but the prices were affordable for all pay grades.

Being an E-3 and an entitled patron of the Commissary I asked around at the hospital just how the Commissary and Exchange came to be?

It was explained to me that both were to help the people in the lower pay grades. No tax, plus they carried items in bulk and sold at a retail price much less than the civilian chain stores charged. The Exchange carried all the basic items needed to keep good health and maintain your Navy requirements in good order.

Smokes were cheap. How about those Sea Stores? One dollar a CARTON!

What happened to the druggist? He's coming back! Sea Stories bounce around, you allude to your best shot and that's no shit!

Did it bother me that when I was standing in line with my full cart, easing up to the register and some and an officer in uniform steps in front of me. Did he have the duty or was he using his gold stripes just to piss me off? Duty? Okay. Were in the military and duty is always first. On duty I would have no calms in helping him empty his carriage.

At the Navy Exchange, I often wondered why every officer with the duty showed up during the noon hour?

Man, it is raining, and my car is at the end of the Exchange parking lot! I am going to get soaked! Taking the quickest way, I cut across the twelve empty reserved spaces in front of the store.

Next time you have to walk across an empty lot with snow up to your ass, no it's not an empty lot. Read the signs!!

"RESERVE PARKING!"

Well, that got vented now back to the quaint drug store. There were metal bar like stools, lined along the side, of a marble top counter. You would sit, order the ultimate banana split, and enjoy one of the great experiences of life. I am here to tell you that they don't make banana splits like that any- more. At one time, every drug store in America made banana splits.

When the large chain stores moved in, the soda fountains along with the gigantic banana split vanished. It's possible they went south with the fleet. Do you remember the guy they called a, "Soda Jerk?"

I wish I could have remembered the druggist name; He was caring and expressed it. As the end of the month neared, we would be down to our last few dollars. We would scrape our change together, and I would walk to the drug store, and buy two cans of Similac. The day that I only had money enough to buy one can he took me aside. He always asked about the baby, and when I was going to bring her by. This time was different. He told me to put the can back on the shelf and take what I needed.

"I know you'll pay me, don't worry about it.

Newport people had no idea who we were or where we came from. The most they knew, I was a Sailor who came to Newport. They showed us compassion and caring.

Chapter 10

I had passed the test for third class and was advance to E-4. I could now wear a Navy crow on my uniforms. The advance making me a third-class petty officer meant I had to leave Food Service. Petty Officers were not assigned to work in the galley. I had made so many navy and civilian friends, it was difficult to say goodbye.

Before I left, I spoke to the Lieutenant in his office. I owned up that I was the one that broke his pen set.

Standing up, he grinned.

"I know you did, and I knew that you wouldn't leave without telling me. It was just a pen set, no big deal. You know in the old days I would have been helping put the still together!"

Still grinning, he sat back down at his desk.

"Now get your ass out of here, I don't allow petty officers in the galley."

The day wasn't quite over. We all mustered at Jim Shea's; mourned the passing of another galley rat. Jim Shea's was a small Tavern on the corner of Marlborough St. and West Broadway. Jim's patrons were mostly corpsmen, from the naval hospital, and under age.

Jim Shay, by trade, was a plumber and assigned to work at the Naval Hospital. Every corpsman that patronized his bar had a tab. On payday, Jim would come around to collect his tabs. Age was of no concern, and in fact, I was nineteen years old, when I started my tab.

The story I heard, was that Jim's brother-in-law was a Sergeant on the Newport police force, and his beat just happen to be the Marlborough Street area. During the years that I was a patron, I never once witnessed any law enforcement or Shore Patrol, enter Jim Shay's to check identifications.

Once in a while, things would get a little rowdy. Jim had a ball bat behind the bar. He would give a yell, and slam the bat down on the bar. Things would immediately settle down.

John Curran worked the bar, when Jim was at work, or when the place was mobbed. John was about the easiest going guy there ever was. He was one hell of a nice guy.

You stood at the bar to drink. An old table and a couple of chairs made up the total furniture. The bathroom was unique the commode flushed, but there was no running water to the sink. Just as well as there was no drain pipe. A noted feature, when using the rest room, was that it had no door.

Rhode Island law stated that women could not enter Taverns. Wives would have to stand out side, and knock on the window, to rouse some one's attention. Yes, I have to admit, my wife was a window knocker, once! It never happened again.

Next to Jim's, on West Broadway, was a Chinese Restaurant. The owner often came in, to embellish himself in beer. He was funny, and had a great sense of humor. Jim and John had him believing he was Irish! To prove it, he would sing a bit of, "When Irish Eyes Are Smiling." With his Chinese accent, it would bring tears to your eyes.

{RIP Jim Shay - John Curran}

Chapter 11

Going from Food Service to Physical Therapy, was one awesome change.

Although I wasn't a technician, the work was interesting. I liked the neck stretcher best of all. I could assist, but I could not render treatment on my own.

In the year 1958, President Eisenhower made Newport his summer White House. The Hospital was alerted that a member of the President's staff would be arriving for a Diathermy treatment.

Arriving at the front entrance, he was greeted, by the elite of the hospital staff, from the Captain on down.

Escorted to a treatment room, the Physiotherapist and one of the senior technicians setup his Diathermy treatment.

When they were finished, I was charged to sit in the room as a safeguard, in the event something went wrong.

The minute, I saw him arriving, wearing his Yankee baseball hat; I knew it was Jim Hagerty! I had been sternly warned to sit, and not to speak to the patient for any reason. So I sat there wondering what I should do, when he turned his head, so he was facing me.

With only the two of us in the room I went for it! I mentioned that he once told me, if I ever saw him again, to say hello. He lifted his head, giving me a good look. He asked me where I new him from. I told him that I was his caddie at the Mountain View Hotel. I went on to remind him that he only played two holes, and then we cut through the woods, making our way to the clubhouse. I even brought up the ten-dollar tip. He laughed.

"I remember that club house!"

It was like when I caddied for him, he asked questions about my service in the Navy. He was one hell of a super person, I felt so proud and how lucky I was, to meet him again.

A bell rang on the Diathermy, signaling the end of his back treatment. I notified the physiotherapist, and Miss Rafferty secured the machine and I removed the Diathermy packs. Mr. Hagerty dressed, and then walked out to the hallway into a herd of people, all asking questions and trying to get a few words with him. Holding his arm up for quiet, he turned and got my attention.

I'm not quite sure what he said, but it was words to the effect he wanted me to walk with him. What I do remember is that all eyes were on me, and it was one of the proudest days of my life. When we got to the car, he shook my hand and told me if I ever saw him again to say hello. Thankfully he did not bring up the Boston Red Sox.

You can image the chitchat after he left. Of course, the questions arose on how I would come to know the Presidents Press Secretary. I was tempted to tell them that we played golf together. Once the truth was known, that I was only his caddy, my claim to fame dwindled rapidly. Being enlisted, my credibility was questionable. No doubt, I probably made up the whole story.

(JAMES HAGERTY 1909 -1981)

Chapter 12

My duty nights were spent in the hospital garage. I was designated as the ambulance attendant. Primarily, I was to assist the ambulance driver, and provide medical care, to navy personnel that we were transporting.

The garage had a bunkroom, making us available, anytime during the night. Most of our runs were transporting patients from the hospital or to the airstrip at Quonset Point. The drawback was that Quonset was located on the other side of Narragansett Bay.

Leaving the hospital compound, we would drive along First Street to Long Wharf. The road branched onto Thames Street, bringing us to the ferry landing. There were two ferryboats that made continuous round trips to the Jamestown side of the bay. It wasn't bad, except in the middle of the winter. If you just missed the ferry, you had to wait almost an hour for it to come back. The Newport landing was always congested, as the Police Station was located in the same area.

Being a Corpsman, most of what I was learning, was classified as on the job training. It was a Saturday in the middle of July and hotter than hell. We received a call, to go to Pier Two, on the Naval Base.

A civilian diver, working under the pier, discovered a sailor's body wedged in between two pilings. Extremely unsettled, the diver refused to help with the recovery. Navy divers were called in, and some how freed the body from the pilings. They surfaced with the body and lifted it up onto the pier. Setting the remains down in front of the driver and myself.

The divers gave us a thumb up and left, their job was over.

For the driver, and me it would be our first experience, handling a dead person. The body was wearing blues and wearing a P-coat indicating that he had been under the pier for some time. Retrieving a body bag from the ambulance, we spread it out next to the body. It was hard not to look, but all the skin on his face and his hands were missing. The crabs had given him a skeletal look. We zipped up the bag and lifted him up into the ambulance.

We wasted no time in heading back to the hospital to drop this poor sailor off at the morgue, scrub out the ambulance with disinfectant, and call it a day.

In order to return to the hospital we had to pass through Gate Two, cross over Admiral Kalbfus Road onto Third Street and then a quick right into the hospital compound.

At the gate, the Marine sentry held us up. He received a message, to inform us that we could not transport the body across a public street until the coroner gave us permission. It was hot, and we sat waiting. The smell and odor from the decomposing body was so strong the driver thought he was going to be sick.

We stood outside the ambulance in the sun for over two hours, before the coroner arrived. He took one look in the back of the ambulance, wrote a few notes and then gave us permission to transport the remains across the city street to the hospital. We did it with all the windows down.

The driver, not feeling all that good, backed the ambulance up to the morgue. The door opened, and a First Class Wave stepped out. **(A Sailor Came to Newport)** I had seen her before. She had four hash marks, giving her at least sixteen years of service. She gave the impression of being as tough as nails and probably was. Grabbing the body bag by the sides we eased it out of the ambulance, through the door, and set it down on the steel autopsy table.

I glanced at the Wave, as we were heading for the door. She had on a pair of rubber gloves and a cigarette dangling out of her mouth. She returned my look and motioned me toward the table.

"Open up the bag, so I can see what we got."

She didn't leave the driver out. Looking in the bag, she gave him an order.

"Search his pockets for an ID, and then get him out of those wet blues."

The driver couldn't handle it. Running across the room, he vomited into the deep sink. I was feeling pretty queasy myself.

Her answerer was for him to clean the deep sink up and try and act like a Corpsman."

She didn't wait on the driver but began to search the pockets of the dead sailor. She withdrew a wallet, lit up another cigarette and studied her findings.

It appeared he was from Detroit, Michigan. He had been under the pier, for a good year and a half. The Navy would have him listed him as a deserter. What were the possibilities? Did he slip and fall? Did he take his life? Was he pushed? We would never know. It was hard to believe he would take his own life, by jumping into the frigid ocean water? (A Sailor Came to Newport)

Miss wonderful, had begun removing the wet clothing from the remains. With her cigarette still dangling out of her mouth, nothing, seemed to bother the woman. Still puffing on a cigarette, she conveyed her thanks to us, though a cloud of smoke.

"You two were a big help. Don't worry about puking, it happens to all of us. If this sort of work appeals to you, let me know, and I will do what I can. No doubt he probably did drown. If you want to watch the autopsy, be here at 0900 in the morning.

She had the body in a sitting position and removed his jumper.

Passing through the door we both had the same thought.

"No fucking way."

Chapter 13

It was this time in our lives that we had outgrown our two-room apartment on Second Street and decided to move. We found an ad in the Newport paper, for a three room fully furnished, apartment on Lincoln Street. The owners were Ed and Nora Hole. They were great people; the apartment was clean and well furnished. It was a luxury compared to Second Street. We made friends with Mr. Ring. He serviced and maintained, the multiple soda and beer dispensers found in most of the island restaurants and pubs. I believe that he was Mrs. Holes father. There weren't too many days that went by that he didn't inquire to our well being and offer his help.

Pat Williams and her two children occupied the second floor. She was also a Navy wife and understandably very independent. Her husband was deployed on a Destroyer, for a six-month cruise, in the North Atlantic. My wife and Pat hit it off and became close friends.

It became increasing difficult, getting around without a car. I had to take the bus, hope for a ride, or make the forty-minute walk to the hospital.

Thankfully, from Lincoln Street, we were able to use a baby stroller, and walk to the First National on Broadway.

On the return trip, without fail, we would always stop at Marcucci's sandwich shop. A two-foot sandwich called the Big M went for seven dollars. A couple of Big M's and we would eat well for three days.

During the late sixties, a snowstorm shut most of the city down; we survived, as well as half of Newport, on two-foot long sandwiches from Mariucci's. Damn they were good, the best. In my Navy travels, I never found another sandwich that could equal the two-footer. However, the Blind Man's in the Philadelphia Naval Shipyard came very close. There was always a line and five employees were making sandwiches. My first time in I went to pay for my sandwich, a black man wearing dark glasses took my money.

"Hey, your new, first time in my shop?"

He turned and smiled at me.

"Don't be a stranger!"

I gave him a twenty-dollar bill. Looking straight ahead, he handed me back the correct change.

The sandwich was like heaven. I became a regular.

Chapter 14

Winter brought us one hell of a blizzard. I can remember being knee deep in snow making my way to the hospital. Cars weren't moving, and it would be three to five days before any one moved their car off Lincoln Street.

My old friend Smithy, in personnel, informed me that since I had made Third Class, one of the benefits was eligibility to apply for Navy Housing.

With our daughter growing, we were finding it difficult, at Lincoln Street to continually climb the stairs to the third floor. We made the decision to move only if we could get Naval Housing. We informed the Holes of our intentions; they were most gracious and understanding.

Naval housing, at one time, was a two story building used for enlisted barracks. It was located, just inside Gate Four, on the Naval Station. It was old, but not lacking for a population of field mice. They seemed to like gathering under the kitchen sink. Base Pest Control did a good job in trying to eradicate these unwelcome guests, but they were greatly out numbered.

Although the Base Commissary and exchange were within walking distance, it was some distance away to shop outside the base. Plus having to put up with the aggravation of putting up with the Marine sentry at the gate. They insisted on checking your ID's, every time you came in or out, even if it was several times in one day. They would also check the contents of all bags you were carrying. It was obvious they used the rouse, to flirt and scope out the more attractive wives. Little did I know that the day would come and I would be wearing a Marine uniform?

There just was little doubt that we needed transportation. I started putting out inquiries around the hospital for advise on where to buy a used car. Both military and civilian workers had high praise for a used car dealer on West Main Road. The first day I had off I took the bus to West Main Road and located the car lot. If I'm not mistaken, the owners name was George Rose. The name just surfaced out of a very obscure memory. I hope I'm not wrong.

He showed me several cars on the lot but focused in on a 1950 Ford. The cars body was a pretty blue color with a shinny black hood. He related that it was the best damn car on the lot. He had received it from Rogers High School. The car had been used as a project, for students to learn auto repair. It was in very good shape; the engine sounded great, tires were all good, so I asked the eventful question.

How Much?"

I am not sure of his answer, and I can't remember what I paid, but it was under a hundred and fifty dollars. It was all I had!

That car turned out to be one hell of a buy. It ran good, and we made numerous trips to New Hampshire. The town located north of Whitefield is Lancaster. Every year the town officials promote the Lancaster Fair. The fair goes back a long ways and marks the end of the summer for the North Country.

I can remember when I was just a little guy I would stand in the midway watching the Hoochie Coochie dancers, the fat lady would smile at me, and I would pay the twenty-five cents to see the two headed calf.

Lucky Teter's, "Hell Drivers" show, was the main attraction at the fair. Purchasing two tickets, we got good seats high up in the grandstand. Two days before we decided to purchase a Chevy II at a local dealer. My home address was still Whitefield so no sales tax. I got a hundred dollar trade in for the Ford. Unknown to us the dealer sold or gave the car to the Lucky Teter's Show.

We watched as one of Lucky Teter's daredevils, accelerated a 1958 Cadillac Eldorado past the grand- stands, making a complete circle around the racetrack he approached the grandstands from the opposite direction. A cloud of smoke erupted from underneath the back end of the car.

We guessed that he had the Caddy going somewhere between seventy and eighty miles an hour. The smoke stopped as he made his approach to the front of the grandstands. It gave everyone a clear, unobstructed view of the Caddy. Steering his way up an eight-foot ramp, he propelled himself and the Cadillac out into space. There was not a ramp for him to land on. He rode the Caddy over the top of six cars, landed straight down on a blue 1950 Ford with a black hood.

We stayed and watched a wrecker pick up what was left of our car. The weight of the Cadillac on impact had pressed the roof down into the frame. When the Caddy landed the crowd cheered as the driver crawled out of the wreck and jumped to the ground. With everyone in the stands up on their feet cheering, we both felt like we had lost our best friend.

Chapter 15

We arrived back at Gate Four in the middle of the afternoon. Without a doubt, I surmised what was going to happen. The Marine sentry seeing I had no government stickers on my windshield motioned me to the side of the road. I did my best to explain that the car was new that we lived in base housing that he could see from the gate. I wanted to drop my wife and baby off so she could be fed, then go to the pass office and get a base sticker.

He had one reply.

"No sticker, No entry."

We decided that we would take the stroller out of the car, put our daughter in it, and my wife could push her to our quarters and in turn I would go to the Pass Office.

The Sentry waited until we had the baby settled in the stroller. My wife started to push forward when the sentry stopped her and demanded to see her ID. This caused me to become immediately angry. He was watching me closely. If he could get me to show any sign of aggression, I would be put on report for interfering with his duties and no doubt it would be a Captains Mast for me.

My wife was retrieving her ID card when a Navy pickup truck pulled up close to my car. It was the Sergeant of the Guard making his rounds of the entry gates.

He was a Staff Sergeant with three hash marks on his sleeve and a chest full of medals. The Private waved a car through the gate then approached his Sergeant. Before he could speak, the Sergeant was all over his ass. We heard it all.

"What in hell is going on here Private? This is no place to have a car parked, why is the trunk open? I didn't authorize any searches. You have a mother, stroller and baby standing in a very high traffic zone."

The sentry was quick to respond.

He spieled out in a Marine manner my attempt to enter the base with out a proper sticker. He gave permission for them to remove the stroller from their trunk. She wanted to walk the baby to their housing unit. They stated the baby had to be fed. When you arrived I was in the process of checking her ID.

The Sergeant approached me and asked for my ID card. I handed it to him; he turned it over and yelled at the sentry.

"Marine, front and center, let the cars back up."

"You stand beside the Private."

Little did we know we were about to get a dressing down, which neither of us would forget?

"Now Private look at this ID and tell me what you see?"

Taking the ID the Sentry looked it over then handed it back.

"He's in the Navy!"

The Staff Sargent held up the ID to the sentry's face.

"What in the hell is this?"

Taking his finger he pointed to the backside of the card.

"It's a red cross."

"And what does that mean to you?"

Struggling for an answer, he stepped aside and waved several cars through the gate.

"Private settle down; I am not here to find fault with you or the sailor. These medals on my chest are there because a Doc crawled out into enemy fire, bandaged my wounds, and then dragged me back to a safe spot. I had been shot twice, back and leg. After making sure that my wounds were attended to he crawled back into the line of fire to reach another Marine. Had we met, he would have told me, that he was just doing his job. Doing his job saved my life."

He paused for a moment and addressed the sentry.

"Private, my advise to you is to take care of the Doc's because some day they may be taking care of you."

The sentry turned to me and stuck out his hand. I quickly accepted.

As the Sargent was getting back into his truck, he called out to the Private.

"Let them go to their quarters and tell the "Squid" to get a sticker."

It was ironic, but the Private and me became good friends.

I was privileged to have known a fellow Corpsman, stationed at the Naval Station, Newport. His name was Martin Gillespie.

Early 1966, Martin received his orders to report to Camp Lejeune, NC, for further duty with the Fleet Marine Force, Republic of Vietnam.

The rest of us would soon follow. He was easily the most Gun Ho Corpsman the most of us ever knew. If there was anything that Gillespie ever wanted, it was to be a grunt Corpsman, with a Marine Combat Infantry Unit.

MARTIN GILLESPIE HM2/USN
Stationed M2 Dispensary
Naval Station, Newport, RI

As Written:

For extraordinary heroism as a platoon corpsman, 2nd Platoon, Company D, First Battalion, Fourth Marines during Operation TEXAS in the Republic of Vietnam against communist insurgent guerrilla forces on 21 March 1966. While engaged in a search and *destroy mission, the 2nd Platoon came under a Deva-stating volume of accurate small arms, semi-automatic weapons, and heavy caliber machine gun fire from concealed, fortified enemy positions about 75 meters to their front. Observing a Marine wounded as he attempted to knock out the enemy emplacements with a rocket launcher, Petty Officer Gillespie* fearlessly dashed across 30 meters of exposed ground, completely dis-regarding the intense volume of fire. Upon reaching the critically wounded Marine, he quickly began administering life saving aid with calm professionalism. Although the surrounding area was raked continually with increasingly accurate enemy fire, Petty Officer Gillespie continued to work, remaining in the exposed position for several minutes until he had stopped the bleeding, and then, as he began to move the wounded Marine to cover, he was mortally struck by enemy fire. As a result of his expert professional skill and his selfless daring actions, the life of the Marine was saved.* Petty Officer Gillespie **gallantly gave his life for his country.** *(A Sailor Came to Newport)*

**Age 26
East Boston, Massachusetts.**

Six Hundred Thirty Eight Hospital Corpsmen were killed in Vietnam.

Chapter 16

Living on the base took a little doing, but once you got used to the Officers Candidates sounding off during their military drill, it became pretty much routine. I met a neighbor, Francis Flynn who was a First Class Corpsman with five hash marks. Nice guy but he drank all the time. The man was never sober; I was thankful that he lived three units down from us. All he ever wanted was to borrow booze. We would meet again at Camp Lejeune and again in Vietnam.

Then came a week with two unexpected happenings, and one surprise. *First Happening*! I received orders to report to the USS Grand Canyon AD 28. We were fortunate in that the ship's homeport was Newport, RI. *Second Happening*! Notification from the base housing office that MEMQ housing was classified as sub-standard, and was slated to be demolished. *Surprise!* The doctor told my wife she was with child.

The housing office issued a list of available housing in the vicinity of the naval base that was available for immediate occupancy. Being far down on the list and of lower rank, I did not qualify for government housing. The office receptionist recommended that I looked into Newport Housing.

Because of my transfer, time was of the essence. I explained my situation and told her I would fully accept her advice. She was kind enough to call the Newport Housing Authority and set me up with an appointment for the next day with the director.

I arrived promptly on time. Entering the housing administrative building several minutes ahead of schedule. I was taken to the office of the director's secretary. I was welcomed with a handful of paperwork to complete. When I was finished, I handed it all back to her. She skimmed through the pages then pressing her intercom button she announced that I was there for my appointment. A voice came back asking her to show me in and to bring in the paperwork.

A medium built man with gray hair stood as I entered and pointed to a chair for me to take a seat. Shuffling through my papers, he glanced through most of them and then set them aside.

"My name is Sam Dawley; I make it a point to meet with everyone applying for public housing. We consist of Park Home, Chapel Terrace and Tonomy Hill. When you came up the hill from Gate 4, you would have passed rows of similar housing with coal bins outside each door."

I nodded that I had noticed them.

"That is the Tonomy Hill Project. At present, we have a mix of civilian and navy tenant's. It's imperative that you all get along. You are responsible for your unit, and that includes the outside grounds. Both are to be kept clean. You will have two trash cans assigned to your unit. They are to be kept to the right side of your front steps. The only exception being the day your trash is picked up. Once your cans are emptied you are to remove them from the curb immediately. Loose trash cans have a tendency to roll with the wind and end up against someone' car. The city is not responsible for damages, but you are! No loud noise or any other loud sound coming from your unit that can disturb your neighbors."

I sat quietly as I listened to him quote rules and regulations.

"Common sense prevails. If you cause problems, you can expect to deal with me. I handle all problems personally and in your case, if I have to talk to your commanding officer, I would do just that."

He handed me a fifteen-page contract containing all the Housing Authority's rules and regulations.

"Read that over and sign it, and then give it to the lady at the front desk. I have a unit ready for occupancy. It's at 72 Mahon Street. Your rent will be sixty-five dollars a month, which includes all utilities. When you give the lady the sixty five dollars she will give you the key, and you're free to move in."

We both stood, and he shook my hand.

"The rent is due on the first of every month. There is a grace period of three days. The fastest way out of here is not to pay your rent."

We moved in over the weekend; the tras h cans were delivered that Monday! This was our first unfurnished apartment. We purchased a bed, nightstands and two bureaus and maybe a couch from Newport Furniture. Contributions from our parents, relatives and friends were all so generous in helping us set up house keeping.

Once we were settled in we went shopping for a television set. They were all big bucks and non-affordable. Because we had no established line of credit, most appliance stores, including Sears were understandable, but we just didn't meet their criteria for credit.

We noted televisions sets in the window of the Goodrich store on upper Broadway. I believe the manager or owner was a Mr. Wright. The salesman was top shelf; His name could have been Martin, I will try to find out.

He sold us a very nice color television set. We did sit down with Mr. Wright, and came up with at sum that we could afford. He made up a payment plan, and we had a television. We never missed a payment and continued to shop there. We had a brand new color television set in our living room, but the only color program being broadcasted was, "Shell Golf."

We met a lot of great people on Mahon Street and over time made a multitude of friendships. Some we would never forget. Cathy Demello, Louise Miller, Jack and Barbara Armstead. It might have been called a project, but our kids were warm, we had electricity and running water, a two-floor apartment and a clean, efficient kitchen. We indeed were fortunate. The kids played outside without worry; no one was trying to sell them drugs. Police were around but seldom seen.

Later, in time, the Navy would relocate the Newport fleet to southern ports. With the fleet gone a multitude of civilian jobs were lost. It resulted in a sudden exodus of both navy and civilian families leaving Newport. It also left an over abundance of empty units in the Tonomy Hill project. The Housing Authority in order to survive had to move people in. They adopted a plan to relocate people from the Chad Brown projects in Providence to Tonomy Hill in Newport. Now there were drugs, stealing, robberies, assaults, drunkenness, child abuse just to name a few. Cops could be seen day and night.

What to do? The answer was to cough up several million dollars tear the buildings down and replace them with modern, affordable living units. It was done, and it was one hell of an improvement. I just wonder where the derelicts, riffraff, and drug dealers all went? Could they still be living there?

Chapter 17

I reported aboard the USS Grand Canyon, AD28, at the Naval Piers Newport, in May of 1961. The ship would be my home for the next three years.   The   ship   was moored against Pier One, with four Destroyers tied a long side.   The Grand Canyon was a repair ship. The interior of the ship housed every possible trade shop needed to make repairs, overhaul, and manufacture new parts. Crewmembers were trained as a specialist in a particular repair field and assigned to shops according to that expertise.

There were three other Destroyer Tenders assigned to Newport. The Yosemite AD19, Cascade AD16, and the Arcadia AD23. A long side each were six to eight destroyers, undergoing routine and emergency repairs.

Being a Corpsman, I was assigned to the Medical Department, commonly known as, "Sick Bay." The department consisted of eight corpsmen, a Chief corpsman and a Medical doctor.

A standing joke among fleet sailors was that the Tenders were welded to the pier, and never went to sea. I had no longer settle in, when I got the news the ship was leaving in August for a six-month cruise to the Mediterranean.

The word was that after we returned to Newport the Grand Canyon would stand down for a period then return for a second cruise. There was no official word confirming that cruise; it was mostly scuttlebutt. Ask any Sailor and he will tell you scuttlebutt was a medium that let the crew know what in hell was going on.

Not being a combat type ship the scuttlebutt was that the Tender would spend most of its time moored to the sea wall in the bay of Naples, Italy. That would prove to be an accurate statement. There was also scuttlebutt about the possibility of the ship visiting Greece, Spain, and the French Riviera.

It was with great difficulty that I informed my wife of the up coming deployment to the Mediterranean. Although we had discussed the hardships of a Navy life, she was not ready to accept my leaving. She asked me to make an appointment with the base Chaplain or the Captain of the Grand Canyon to explain that she was pregnant, and I was needed at home. I reminded her of the Navy wives she had known. They had children, were pregnant and their husbands were at sea. I got no response.

I let her dwell on it for a few days. We were talking but never about the deployment. I went back and forth to the ship everyday and had the duty every third day and every third weekend. Time was slipping by, and I had to get the situation resolved.

That night we went for hamburgers at Carrols Drive In, on West Main Road. Our daughter loved the place, and while she was devouring her burger, I mentioned the date the ship was leaving.

I knew she was afraid to be alone. I brought up the possibility that if she felt safer, she could stay with her parents and have the baby at the Whitefield Hospital. Her mother would certainly be a big help. Champus would pay the expenses. As far as the apartment, I would inform the housing office that my ship was leaving, and you would be visiting your parents.

She was quiet for a few minutes, then started making a few changes of her own to my suggestion. On our return to Mahon Street, she was immediately on the phone to her mother. From what I could gather her mother was all for it. Yippee!

All went according to plan. My wife and daughter stayed with her parents in Dalton. Right on schedule my wife gave birth at the Morrison Hospital in Whitefield. That made two of us alumni of the hospital.

My wife was born in her grandparent's house in Dalton. Upon the arrival of the Grand Canyon back in Newport, I would have a wife and two daughters to greet.

Chapter 18

We left Newport right on schedule. The tugs pushed the ship out away from the pier and into the deep-water channel. The ships engines took over, and one could feel the ship come alive under its power. It was my first experience of being aboard a large ship. Prior to the Navy, the largest boat I had ever been on was a "row" boat to go fishing.

We stood at attention, on the outside decks, in dress uniforms until we were dismissed. Passing by Castle Hill I felt the loneliness of leaving my wife behind and all that was important to me. I was on a ship at sea, full of anxiety on what the future would bring.

Once we were out of sight of land the Boson blew his pipe, dismissing the ships crew from quarters. I learned to listen to the "old salts," that the ships speed ranged from ten to fourteen knots and that it would take us twelve to fourteen days to cross the Atlantic, to the Rock of Gibraltar.

I had met all the other corpsmen and felt comfortable about fitting in. Sick Bay was divided up into several compartments. As the specialist in the repair shops, sickbay was operated in the same fashion. Five of the corpsmen had attended and graduated from schools involving their specific fields. Our sickbay had a Laboratory, X-ray, Operating Room and a Pharmacy Technician.

Duty aboard the Grand Canyon turned out to be the foremost learning experience of my Navy career. I was assigned to work with each technician for two months to become proficient in the various aspects of his specialty. If the circumstances ever warranted, I would have the basic skills to stand in wherever needed.

My first assignment was working in X-ray. I learned quickly and became quite proficient in the use of the X-ray machine. In the darkroom came detailed safety instructions in the handling of chemical solutions with strict adherence to follow. I spent a lot of time on the techniques of film developing. I became quite proficient in reading wet films. The best part of the darkroom was I could hang a small sign on the outside of the door, stating that the darkroom was in use. I would slide the inside lock bolt to close and get a thirty minute nap with out a problem.

I enjoyed my tour in the treatment room. I was able to work side by side with the Medical Officer. I learned to suture wounds, prescribed medicines and recognize various medical conditions. Nothing came prepackaged, or disposable. At the end of the day, needles had to be sharpened, syringes, and surgical instruments washed then re-packed, into various surgical packs, then autoclaved for their next use.

The Pharmacy was somewhat different than what I expected. Everything was made, bottled and packaged. There were no pre-packaged cough syrups; we made our cough syrup. The most popular was "ETH." The crew held it in high esteem, the reason might have been, that its main ingredient, was one hundred ninety proof alcohol

Having a limited background in mathematics, I found it difficult and often impossible in understanding complex formulas and measurements.

A major accomplishment, even with my limited background, I was able to formulate, how to make Gin and Vodka.

By this time, we were well into the med cruise and without a doubt working with the Lab Tech was my favorite. The microscope and I became immediate friends.

The world of good and bad microorganisms was the Laboratory technician's forte. The procedure that brought out my sense of humor was the Gram Stain. A bit of specimen would be spread on a clean blank slide, followed by the application of various dyes. Dried and covered with a cover slide, it would be transported to the microscope.

I couldn't wait to focus in. Yes! It was another winner. In my best handwriting, I would write the findings on a lab chit and send it to the Doctor.

"Gram negative diplococci, intra and extracellular, morphologically resembling Neisseria gonorrhea."

Observing the complete procedure, having no idea what was going on, the young sailor would ask?

"I've been lifting some real heavy cargo do you think it caused a strain?"

In his best professional bed side manner, the doctor would answer.

"No it's not a strain, it's the clap!"

(The Clap," which is derived from the French word "clair," meaning brothel)

Chapter 19

Crossing the ocean the weather constantly changed. The swells rocked the ship back and forth like a giant cradle. It was especially rough when the doctor diagnosed a crewmember with acute appendicitis. As a rule appendix are not removed at sea, but rather antibiotics are administered in high doses and the area around the appendix packed in ice until reaching port and a hospital. Although we were at the three-quarter mark of our crossing, the doctor deemed it an emergency.

The Operating Room Tech. readied the instruments while the rest of us got the room ready. The Captain changed the ships course so the ship would ride as smooth as possible. The operation was a success. After cleanup we gathered to see the doctors trophy. It couldn't be found! Was it normal or did it burst? It could never be disputed. It was lost! I've always had the feeling that some how; it found its way over the side.

Mediterranean

Tied up to the sea wall in Naples, the ship fell into a routine. There were six ships anchored in the bay needing repairs, plus a destroyer tied along side us. Basically, the Medical Department held sick call for the crew, monitored ships sanitation and conducted physicals on personnel being discharged from the Navy.

I was assigned to the Fleet Landing, as the duty corpsman. Visiting Navy ships were anchored at various locations inside the Bay of Naples. Ammo ships, Oilers, and Aircraft Carriers were anchored well out past the sea wall, for safety and the carriers need for deeper water.

The Fleet Landing was where ships dropped off and picked up their liberty parties using their ships small craft, commonly called liberty boats.

When a boat left the landing for its ship, a trip out and back could take up to an hour. A sailor just missing his boat had no choice but to wait at the landing for a boat to return.

It was common for sailors, waiting for their boats, to be half shit faced and looking for trouble. There was no age limit on drinking so state side minors took full advantage. Then there was the rivalry existing between ships leading to sudden outbreaks of hostilities and injures.

Six to eight shore patrols were assigned to the landing to keep the peace. Imagine twenty intoxicated sailors waiting for their boats. They have been drinking, all night and there are no facilities at the landing. They have to go! Things get ugly! Most of the time the Shore Patrol would find a near by Italian facility to ease the problems. Then there is always the sailor who will stand on the landing dock and urinates into the bay.

When hostilities break out, they try to calm everyone down rather than use force. On the other side of the coin there are some who are so belligerent, combative and aggressive from the use of alcohol they are in grave danger of hurting themselves or those around him.

This is where I make my entrance. First of all, the Shore Patrol takes control of the situation, by dragging the sailor to the ground and holding him there. I inject a dose of Sparine into the bad boys arm.

It works rather fast but if it doesn't calm his aggression down, then step two he is restrained with the use of a straight jacket. If he is still combative, he is confined in a wire mesh stretcher. Commonly called a Stokes stretcher, widely used in the military. Using restraint straps he is secured to the inside of the stretcher.

The last procedure to be used is to place a second stokes over the top of the first stretcher. The two then are bound together. The sailor is incapacitated and immobilized inside a wire cage. Put aboard a liberty boat and sent back to his ship.

It was a good system. It protected anyone from getting hurt plus eliminating the possibility of self-injury. The risk involved was in transporting the stretcher by boat. The logistics of hoisting it aboard, opened the possibility the stretcher could be accidently dropped. There would be no likelihood of rescue.

Did these situations really occur? "Every Night!" We made a trip to Greece. Just before liberty call the word was passed through out the ship, not to drink the "**Ouzo**." It could cause erratic behavior and uncontrollable aggression. What happened? Two hundred sailors on liberty went looking for Ouzo!

Chapter 20

We made a trip to a port in northern Italy. I think was LaSpezia, but I'm not sure. We had a make shift landing setup to land our liberty boats. Being the only ship in port we had one Shore Patrol on watch. It was like a picnic compared to Naples.

I had only been on medical watch for a couple of hours when a Navy sedan sped up along side of the landing. The driver, a Navy Lieutenant, was first out of the car. Following behind him on his heels was a Navy Ensign. They went directly to the Officer on duty. A few minutes later he approached me. There was an emergency, and I was to go with the Lieutenant. Grabbing my bag, I got into the back seat of the sedan. I had no idea where I was going or what I would find.

The Lieutenant was driving and not wasting any time. I noticed he was looking at me in his rear view mirror.

"Doc, I'm from the Navy Lesion office. The Ensign here is a crewmember on the Aspro that left two days ago for Naples. The Ensigns wife has been following ship from port to port. A few days ago she became ill; the Ensign got permission to stay with her.

Speeding a long the narrow streets he dropped the bomb on me.

"We are almost to the hotel. She believes it is possible that she is having a miscarriage.

I sat in the back seat completely caught off guard. I was dumbfounded that they would leave the Ensign's wife alone in a hotel room, in a foreign country while hemorrhaging. She could be lying there bleeding to death while they raced across town to get a Third-Class Corpsman.

I had just turned twenty years old; miscarriages were not in the curriculum at Corps School. I would do what I could, and that would have to be it.

"Doc, this is the hotel, if you think she needs immediate care we can have an ambulance transport her to a hospital in Germany. It's around one hundred and fifty miles from here. Give the word, and she's on her way."

We left the car, crossed the lobby, and took the lift to the second floor. On the way the Lieutenant whispered to me that under no circumstances would the Ensign let any Italian doctor go near his wife.

Outside their door, it was decided that the two of them would wait in the hall while I proceeded into the room alone. Inside I found a very young scared woman, maybe a few years older than me. I went to her bedside with my bag and took her vital signs. I can't remember what they were, but I know I was not happy with her blood pressure. Embarrassed as hell, I told her that I would have to see just how much she was bleeding. She nodded her consent; I saw enough to pull the sheet back up.

I sat down on a chair that was next to the bed. I told her I was not trained or qualified to handle or treat her condition. I emphasized that I had enough training to know when it was time to get a doctor.

We had to get a doctor and soon. She responded that her husband would not allow it. She would have to go to Germany. I leaned toward the bed to get as close to her as I could.

"Your blood pressure is erratic. When your husband comes, have him, remove the blood soaked pads and replace them with the clean pads. Use the strings to hold them in place, so they act as a pressure bandage. You will be more comfortable having your husband do it."

I stood to leave the room, turned and sat down. A concerned look crossed her face from not knowing what I was going to say. Not meaning to scare her I decided not to say anything. I smiled and left the room.

The two officers were waiting in the hall. As I emerged the Ensign pushed by me and went into the room. I shut the door and addressed the lieutenant.

"Sir, her bleeding is increasing and her blood pressure causes me to worry. You have to get a doctor, like now!"

He nodded, repeating that the Ensign would not allow an Italian doctor near her.

Checking his watch he calculated the time it would take to travel to the hospital in Germany. Finished he looked to me.

"I have to leave; I got to see if we have an ambulance available and if not see where I can rent one, it will take some time."

Not before I had my say.

"Lieutenant, I might not have a lot of experience with a situation like this, but I am positive of one thing. If you put her in an ambulance for a one hundred and fifty mile trip, without a doubt, she will miscarriage along the way. Out on the road there will be little or no way to stop the hemorrhage, my guess is, she will probably die."

He looked at me very concerned.

"What to hell do you want me to do? Pull rank on the Ensign?

Being a low rated enlisted man it is difficult to convince a Naval Officer that he is wrong.

"Lieutenant Sir, if she stays any longer in the hotel room I believe she will miscarriage and maybe die. A hundred and fifty mile ride in an ambulance she will without a doubt miscarriage. Out on the road there is no way to control the hemorrhage and she will die.

Before he could interrupt me, I finished what I had to say.

"Do you know how many babies have been born in Italy since the Roman days? If any country had doctors, expert in childbirth, it has to be Italy. You have to do what ever it takes to get the Ensign to act, or he is going to place his wife in serious jeopardy."

Giving me a nod of understanding, the Lieutenant nodded, stepped into the room and closed the door.

I could hear a muffled discussion going on, when the door opened, and the Lieutenant was smiling.

"Go below to the main desk. Convince them that she is having a baby, and we need a doctor, pronto."

As I started down the hallway, he had something to add.

"When the Doctor gets here they both want you to be present in the room to observe."

Double-timing it down the stairs, I just couldn't believe it.

"You people can't be serious; a Third Class Corpsman is going to watch over the Doctor to make sure he does it right."

The Doctor was a middle-aged man, well dressed and indeed professional looking. His downfall was he could speak little English. He checked her blood pressure and became very concerned over the amount of blood she was loosing.

He tried explaining, to no avail. The Ensign asks me, like I should know, what the doctor was saying. Between sign language and a little body English, he wanted to take her to the hospital at once.

Again the Ensign raised a fuss. He would only agree if I went with them.

An ambulance was called and shortly there after we arrived at the hospital. It was a modern facility with a very professional staff. All went very well and very shortly she was out of danger and the hemorrhage under control.

The Lieutenant gave me a ride back to the landing just in time for me to catch the last liberty boat to the ship. Shaking my hand, he expounded on the good job I had done.

The next morning we left for Naples, and the incident was forgotten. I had to brief the Chief on what went down. He laughed and told me that the Lieutenants report to sixth fleet would be all him and no mention of a corpsman. Just the way it is.

Chapter 21

We were down to the last few weeks of our deployment. I couldn't wait until I could hold my family in my arms. I often thought of how my wife was doing in Dalton. A town with only one streetlight. An exciting happening is to see a Moose in the front yard.

I passed my time by walking along the top of Mr. Vesuvius, strolling through Pompeii, climbing to the top of the leaning Tower of Pisa, taking a boat ride through the Blue Lagoon on the Isle of Capri, confined to the ship while Lucky Luciano was paraded through the streets of Naples, and being a top shelf ping pong player at the Naples Seaman's club. I even made it to St. Peters Square on Easter Sunday to view Pope John celebrate mass.

A substantial amount, of the thousands of sailors, which walked the streets of Newport, had followed the same itinerary. There would be some that even remembered the Campfire girls!

On the trip back across the Atlantic, we met with a storm so forceful that it tore chained vehicles off the decks and flung them into the sea. The ship was rolling at such a degree water was pouring though the supposed water tight portholes on the main deck. Every loose object had to be tied down or else they became instant missiles. Soup and peanut butter sandwiches were the menu of the day.

I was kept busy helping out in the lab with crew members, thinking they had a venereal disease. Besides the lab work, in the quest to find a social disease, examination of if the gentiles were also conducted.

It was times like this that my title, "Doc" took a back seat to; Pecker Checker, Shanker

Mechanic, and Penis Machinist. Little did I know that these job titles would follow me for the rest of my life?

The Grand Canyon returned to Pier One in Newport. After a stand down, rest and replenishment it would make a return trip to the Mediterranean.

Chapter 22

With returning home celebrations over, as a family we settled down to a routine way of life. For our family treat, it was down to Thames Street, to the docks and "Johnny Mack's." The fried clams were so big and the french fries so plentiful they were carried to our outside table in a cut down beer box.

They were so good, and the price was affordable. You either took your leftovers home or fed them to a few million sea gulls that were begging for a hand out.

Our all time favorite was "Lincoln Park." We went to see the stars of "Car Fifty-Four Where Are You?" Their performance was great. Who could ever forget Officer Muldoon? The kids would go on the rides; then we would sit in the food section and pig out! We went back several times; it was a great place for families and most of all it was affordable.

On October 22, 1962 President Kennedy announced that the Soviet Union was transporting nuclear weapons to Cuba. He notified the Soviet Union that the United States was taking the necessary action to prevent their delivery to Cuba.

At that time, the word was passed throughout Newport for all hands to report to their ships on the double. The pier was a mass of sailors returning to their ships with every man wondering what in hell was going on. Civilian equipment operators along with Navy working parties were loading pallets of stores aboard each ship. Once their stores were aboard, and the crew accounted for, they got underway.

Aboard the Grand Canyon, the word was passed that we were not to reveal our destination or the purpose of our mission. We were not to discuss the ships movement with family, relatives or friends. I couldn't tell my wife anything. Hell I didn't know anything.

The Grand Canyon got underway still shielded in mystery. The scuttlebutt was that we were going to war with Russia, putting the wood to Castro, and sending missiles into downtown Moscow. We could be gone a long time, maybe years! It was very scary. We were on the verge of a full-scale war. The Grand Canyon was not outfitted to pursue the enemy but because it kept war ships on the line it was a prime target.

When the ship was well out to sea, the Captain addressed the crew. President Kennedy had ordered a blockade to Intercept Russian ships headed for Cuba. It was a wait and see to what the Russian would do. If they refused to change course offensive action would be taken by the United States. Orders for the Grand Canyon were to proceed to San Juan, Porto Rico.

It was unbelievable that while the entire Naval fleet from Newport, Norfolk, Charleston and Mayport, were steaming in the Atlantic and getting ready to kick ass, we were being tied up to the pier in down town San Juan.

Our mission was to supply support for our ships and the ships from those countries that were our allies. The crisis ended a week later when Khrushchev realized the power of the United States and the determination and fortitude of President Kennedy.

Chapter 23

The first ship to moor along side was an old American destroyer that had been given to the Dominica Republic. We put rat guards on all the lines between the two ships as it was rumored that they might have rodents on board.

As soon as the lines were secured two or three Dominium Republic sailors took positions on their main deck, straight across from our main deck. Each man was caring a type of machine gun, resembling a Burp Gun.

What could they have on board, that they didn't want us snooping around. They had nothing on board and the rumor was the men posted with arms were to keep anyone from trying to leave the ship. That was hard to believe but who knows.

The next two ships were from Argentina. They were former World War Two German destroyers. Both ships and their crews stood equal to ours. The shape and outline of the ships gave thought to when they might have battled our ships and submarines during World War II.

San Juan was beautiful. We frequented the public beach and swam in complete safety. An underwater net provided protection from Barracuda's and Sharks. The net would keep the big fish out of the swimming area but still allowed for schools of smaller fish to enter and leave at will. Using a snorkel you could swim through schools of the most colorful fish in the world.

With the crisis over, the Grand Canyon began to ready for the return trip to Newport. Before leaving a small contingent of the crew, were faced with their own crisis. Boarding buses they left the ship for a tour of the Bacardi Rum factory. During the tour, they were each offered their favorite rum drink using Bacardi Rum. This part of the tour went well. Other than a few tea-drinkers all hands were in a mellow mood. At the end of the tour and just before boarding the bus, each sailor was given a pint of Bacardi's Rum as a gift.

This presented a second lesser know crisis on a bus in downtown San Juan. A first-class Boiler Tender (A Sailor Came to Newport) with twenty-three years of service presented three probabilities. (1) They could chug –a-lug the pint on the short ride back to the ship, however arriving back sick and shitfaced. (2) Although it is against Naval Regulations to bring alcohol aboard ship you could fit the pint in your waist ban and cover it with your jumper. (3) Give the pints to the civilian bus driver.

Conclusion! We are dealing with White Hats, your sons, the pride of your lives, your little boy. Each man stepped down from the bus, stumbled and walked up the gangway. Saluted the colors and reported aboard. They were ordered to lift their jumpers upward and let their belt line be searched. Nothing was found. The bus driver received not one pint. The floor of his bus was strewed from one end to the other with empty Rum bottles. "Crisis, what crisis?"

Chapter 24

The time spent on the Grand Canyon was very productive in learning my rate. I had been advanced to E-5 and was now a Second Class Petty Officer. There was little future for me to make a decent living if we returned to New Hampshire. We decided to stay with the security of the Navy. I re-enlisted aboard the Grand Canyon for four more years.

As my transfer date approached I received orders to the Navy Preventive Medicine School, Oakland Naval Hospital, Oakland California. The school was for six months and upon completion, once again we would receive orders for further transfer.

The orders transferring me to California for six months brought about a serious dilemma. Should my family stay in Newport, on the chance I would be transferred back to New England? It was a possibility or did we pack up the car and head west?

After much decision making, we decided that we would all hit the road. Never driving south of Rhode Island we were filled with apprehension for the long road ahead?

Things went pretty smooth. We gave our notice at the housing office and made arrangements for the navy to have our household goods packed up and shipped to California.

It was very hard to say goodbye to our friends. We had become very attached to Newport. A final trip around Ocean Drive and we headed north to say goodbye to the parents.

A friend of my father-in-law was waiting to see me. He held up two heavy canvas bags while relating that he had driven across the Great Salt Lake Desert several times.

"There is not one thing out there. The distance is a good hundred miles, and the sun is unmerciful. If your car, overheats your in a world of trouble."

Motioning me to the front of my car he pointed out where he was going to attach hooks that would hold the water bags safely above the front bumper. My instructions were to put the canvas sacks in the trunk until I got to the desert. Once there I was to stop at a gas station, get the bags filled with water and hang both on the front of the car.

The time came that we finely reached Utah and the Great Salt Lake Desert. I followed my instructions to the letter. The fellow at the garage was not so enthused, but filled the bags with water and helped me attach them to the front of the car. Looking at the car plates he just kept shaking his head.

As we approached the desert, you could see the road stretched out ahead for miles. Our surprise was that there was water on both sides of the road as far as you could see? Mile upon mile nothing but water.

We drove over the Donner Pass and made our way through Sacramento and on to Oakland. It had been a long drive ending as we drove through the main gate of the Oakland Naval Hospital.

I had NH plates on my car. In those days, the plates were lettered by what county you lived in. Whitefield and Dalton were in Coos County, so my plate started with the letter "O."

The gate sentry directed me to the Preventive Medicine School, which was located at the far end of the compound. As we pulled into the parking lot, the car I parked along side of had NH plates with the starting letter "O." How wild is that?

Inside the office I found out that his name was Leo Therreian and he was from Berlin, NH. We both had orders to the same school!

It took less than an hour for me to complete the check in process and give my wife a smoke break. I was given an in-depth itinerary that covered every aspect of my being for the next six months. It included directions to Naval housing that was located a few miles from Pleasanton and approximately twenty-five miles from Oakland. We had received the keys and the address of a unit, along with reading material on all the do's and don'ts. Our household effects had arrived and would be delivered the next day. A big plus for us was the low monthly rent.

Being a long day and very tired, we decided to find a Motel on the way to Pleasanton. The girls, plus ourselves needed a good meal, shower and a good nights sleep.

Early the next morning we had breakfast, then set course for our new home.

The sign on the entrance road read.

"Welcome to Komandorski Village. U.S. Naval Housing

We had pictured in our minds what our new home might look like; we couldn't have been more mistaken.

Komandorski Village consisted of vintage two-decker World War II, Army barracks. The Navy had converted them into temporary housing. Each building housed four apartments. Two units top side and two at ground level.

The Navy's objective was to provide suitable housing for personnel attending Navy schools in the Oakland area. By providing living quarters, it relieved the stress of new arrivals having to find short time housing for their families.

We were moved into a second-floor unit having a picturesque view of the rolling hills that bordered us behind the housing. I often thought that one day I would see a herd of Buffalo stampeding down from the hills.

Chapter 25

The following morning I car-pooled to my first day of school.

The classes were tough going; it began with Parasitology, Entomology and Bacteriology. Throw in Pest and Rodent control along with several Sanitation courses made my day. In my spare time, I was to learn the genus and order of every mosquito and flea roaming the universe.

The event that compelled me to leave my beer in the refrigerator and pad lock the door was when the school issued out a "slide rule."

The Navy had a way of making you study. Flunk out and your on the next destroyer leaving for a three-year tour in the Orient. I can honestly say I never studied so hard in my life.

During the week, I saw little of my family. I would get home from school, eat dinner and disappear into the bedroom to study. The days were trying for all the wives and the children as well.

Inside the village was a small convenience store. On our first visit, the owner of the store detected our accents. It led to that he was from Lincoln, New Hampshire. My wife was thrilled as her Grandfather and Grandmother both lived in Lincoln. Growing up she had spent a lot of time visiting them. Lincoln became an on going discussion between the two of them for our entire six-month stay.

We had a few non-class days where we had field trips away from the school. Our first trip was to Berkeley University Laboratory facilities where they had developed a procedure that under the microscope, the spirochete causing Syphilis was identified using ultra-violet lighting.

Our next field trip was to the Swift Meat Packing trip in San Francisco. We arrived early morning in the area of the plant dealing with the processing of chickens. Two eighteen wheeler flat beds had crates stacked eight high and six across crammed full of chickens.

As the crates were removed from the truck, workers would remove the chickens and hang them upside down on a revolving wire. You can guess the noise level. As they moved away from the truck, several other workers would grab hold of their heads and slit their throats. The blood would drip into stainless steel troth. The blood would be processed and later sold to dog food company, or consumer sales for the making of chicken blood rice, chicken blood sausage, blood pancakes and blood soups, stews and sauces.

Nearing the end of the troth, the chicken bled to death. A large machine sat waiting. The chickens are pulled, using the same wire, into the machine. They come out at the far end, plucked!

From Chicken Little, our next stop was the stockyards. Using electric probes they would force several cattle into an enclosed pen closing the gate behind them. The fencing was electrified and moved on tracks. The fence would slowly close in around the cattle squeezing them against each other. When they couldn't move a worker carrying an air gun, walked across their backs. As he did so, he would place the tip of the air gun to the top of each livestock's head and pull the trigger. All that was heard was the pop of loud air.

The enclosure was moved back and as it did so the cattle fell dead. They were immediately lifted off the ground using chain and tackle. By means of an overhead rail, they were pulled into the Skinner's area.

This was the only part of the tour we were not allowed to observe. Heavy canvas drop curtains cordoned off the area. Our guide told us that Skinners were very temperamental and did not want visitors watching them skinning the animals. He also mentioned that

Skinners had the highest suicide rate in the world.

From the Skinners area, the cattle are cut into sections. Doctors examined the internal organs to ensure the animal is disease free. The tour went on and on, but not wanting to bore you any longer let me say that the Pigs and the Sheep were electrocuted and at the end of the tour we got a free hot dog!

The last field trip to mention were individual visits to various city Health Departments. All were within driving distance of the hospital. I was assigned to spend two days in San Jose. I left early in the morning trying to beat the traffic to no avail. I arrived at the San Jose Health Department just in time to be checked in. I met the Director and his assistant. After a short speech on how glad they were to be able to assist the Navy. With the formalities over I was assigned to spend the next two days with, let's call him Dave,

Dave was to teach me the ways of a health inspector. I would say Dave was in his late twenties, single and left little doubt that he was a "steamer." Regardless, we got along exceptionally well.

At lunchtime, Dave thought we should check out a pizza parlor. He also left the inspecting up to me. He introduced him self to the manager, showed him his credentials, and informed him that as a new member of the team I would be making the inspection. The manager was uptight. The last thing he needed was a couple of bozos from the Health Department holding an inspection.

I have to admit that the inspection went well. The preparation area was exceptionally clean, and I informed the manager to that fact.

Dave was sitting in a booth and motioned me to join him. Looking past me, he caught the attention of the manager.

"You know it's so close to lunch time we are going to order a couple of pizza's and a pitcher of coke."

The manager elated over the inspection results was quick to give us menus. After we had finished eating, Dave went to the cash register to pay. The clerk told him the manager had taken care of it. We left.

It was just a beautiful California day, and I wondered why we were leaving the city and driving to the suburbs.

"Here's the plan. All these people living here are well heeled. As you can see, the houses are in the big dollar category."

I was impressed, how did they ever get so much money.

"Here's the plan, as we past the houses you look for swimming pools. If you see men, we keep on rolling."

Without warning Dave pulled into the driveway and parked. Through a chain   length fence, we could see a very attractive lady, wearing a skimpy two-piece bikini, lying on an opened lounge chair.

Dave opened the walk through gate and stepped into the pool area. Flashing his Identification he raised his voice and called out across the pool.

"We are from the State Health Department, here to inspect your pool."

She was upset because in the last ten years no one had inspected the pool before. With an explanation of there being over three thousand pools in San Jose alone, ten years was just about right.

She seemed to accept his reasoning and stood up from the lounge chair. She made no effort to cover herself. Dave made a quick inspection of the pool never taking his eyes off her. She merely looked away. He approached her with deep concerns over his findings. The filter operation and the chlorinator were both outdated which increased the probably of high bacteria counts which could lead to disease bearing organisms. He would have to take samples and bring them to the lab. The pool might have to be emptied and closed.

The woman was deeply concerned and kept looking at her pool asking what could she do? I had no answers; David flipped a couple of pages on his clipboard, announcing he would have to walk back to his car to retrieve his pen. She offered him the use of a pen. It was just inside the kitchen.

Back at the school, when asked how my day went? I had one answer!

"I learned a lot."

Chapter 26

School was winding down. We had final exams scheduled for the last week. The real difficult and demanding part of the exam was in the lab. Twenty microscopes were placed on each desk. Looking into each microscope we had to make identification and correctly spell our findings. To make it interesting one of the microscopes was bogus.

The week over we were all notified that we had all passed, and no one would be put on a slow boat to China! We were given certificates and notations made in our service records that we were now classified as Preventive Medicine Technicians

I had exciting news to take home. I could hardly contain myself as I gathered everyone in the living room. I announced that I was officially a Navy Preventive Medicine Technician. I got a nice round of congratulations with my wife leading the hand clapping.

It was then that I dropped the bomb!

"By the way, I got my orders I'm being transferred to the Naval Dispensary, U.S. Naval Station, NEWPORT, Rhode Island.

All hell broke loose.

We were jumping for joy over receiving orders to Newport. It took half the night for us to settle down.

The following day I immediately contacted the housing authority, explaining that I had received orders for Newport. We would be arriving within the next thirty days. I gave the secretary my name and our previous address on Mahan Street. I was surprised when she remembered whom I was and if I was looking to move back into Tomony Hill. I was quick to answer in the affirmative. She took my local phone number assuring me she would check into the availability and return my call.

The next morning she called early there was a unit on Mahan Street available. It was not our previous unit but close by. The authority required a one hundred dollar deposit to hold the unit. The deposit would be returned upon our moving in. Assuring her a check would be in the morning mail, I just couldn't thank her enough. The most difficult task for a Navy family with orders to Newport was finding a place to live.

Our household goods were packed and shipped to Newport. I graduated from

Preventive Medicine School, packed the car to the roof, including the roof, sat the girls in the back seat and headed east on Route 66.

We waited at our parent's home in New Hampshire until we were notified our household goods had arrived. We set a date for delivery and left for Newport. Arriving a few days early we checked into the San Castle Motel in Middletown very close to the beach. It gave the kids an ideal place to relax and unwind. The motel was an adventure by itself. A local bar was located just behind the motel. Being a sailor of a few years, I still never had the guts to go in.

When we were settled back in to Mahon Street, I checked in to the Naval Station for duty. I was assigned to M-2 Dispensary, which was centered in between the Dental Clinic and the Law School. The dispensary main function was to hold daily sick call for Military and Civilian personnel attached to the Naval Base. The afternoon was allotted to conducting physical exams of college students applying for Officers Candidate School. The most intense exams were held by the flight surgeon on Officers Candidates qualifying for flight training.

The building resembled the ones in Komandorski Village. Second world war vintage with everything made out of wood. The waiting rooms had beautiful hand carved pews

117

and every counter in the place was stained with multi-coats of varnish. The floors at one time appeared to be oak but over time they had been covered over with black and green tiles.

When you entered the front door, you were at what was called the "front desk." I soon learned that it was the domain of Chief Perry. (A Sailor Came to Newport)*

The Chief ruled! Nothing happened, nothing took place, nothing transpired, nothing came about that the Chief didn't have control of.

He had contacts all over the base both military and civilian. His brother was frequently at the dispensary. He was a civilian worker with an office in public works. I never knew and never asked what position he held. He would spend a lot of time at the Dispensary talking to his brother.

Chapter 27

Passing by the front desk the first office in was my domain. A sharp right and a passageway ran the length of the building. On each side of the passageway were office's identified by signs above the doorways. Two-thirds of the way down the long hallway was the office of Commander Coleman. He was the Administrative Officer, which meant he had the rule over all of us including Chief Perry.

The Commander's claim to fame was he hated noise. Any noise outside his office and he would hold Chief Perry responsible. No matter how hard he tried to keep the noise level down the Commander would chew his ass out two to three times a day. He was paranoia at its best. If you coughed the intercom would come on a familiar voice would beam out.

"Keep the Noise Down."

There was a First Class Corpsman assigned to the physical exam section by the name of Cook. He had taken the exam and was headed for a commission in the Medical Service Corps. Cook had a good friend, a retired chief, who managed the bowling alley located down the street from the dispensary.

(A Sailor Came to Newport)

Cook gets the Chief to give him six old pins and a bowling ball no longer in use.

Using the back entrance door of the dispensary, Cook was located at the end of the passageway that ran past the Commanders office. In complete silence, he set the pins up in a triangle shape. Quietly he left from the rear door. Taking the bowling ball, he ran along the front of the building, through the entrance door, stopped took aim, and lobbed the ball down the passageway. The rumbling sound of the ball rolling down the hallway and then taking out the pins was spectacular.

The Commander flew out of his office. It was amazing that the front of his pants weren't wet. He charged up the hallway yelling for the Chief. There was no one at the front desk or a soul in sight. Becoming frustrated, he slammed his fist on the check in counter.

The door to the men's bathroom opened, and Chief Perry stepped out. The Commander was beside himself.

"Chief who was responsible for this insane act? I want to know right now!"

I was in the Preventive Medicine Office located just off the main entrance. I was out of sight, but I could hear their conversations quite well.

The Chief maintained his cool by keeping his voice inquisitive as he spoke.

"Commander I have been having trouble with my bowels. I was pretty much self-involved. Just what are you referring to?"

Taking the Chief by the sleeve, of his coat he pointed down the passageway.

"Tell me Chief Perry, just who in the hell is going to pick that mess up?"

The Chief looked down the passageway shaking his head.

"Commander, it's a little late in the day but I'll try and locate a pin boy!"

We were all called to general quarters with no one admitting guilt. We were warned, threatened and chewed out. We were dismissed with the knowledge that the Commander would sit back and wait for his turn to pork anyone of us. We all maintained a low profile except for newly appointed Ensign Cook, who was still laughing.

I have to jump up a few years to impart this sea story. I was shopping in a Wal-Mart Super store wearing my Newport, Rhode Island tee shirt. A heavyset man nearing his seventies read the front of my shirt and stopped me.

"A long time ago I was in Newport but just for a few days in the Navy Transit Barracks."

Rolling up his sleeve he showed me a worn out tattoo that read, "FRED."

"A few of us went into Newport and got pretty well liquored up. To this day I don't know where I got the tattoo. Woke up in the morning, and there it was." (A Sailor Came to Newport)

I just can't remember a Tattoo Parlor; it had to be somewhere around Thames Street. A friend told me it was called, "Ruby's?"

Chapter 28

I found myself in the position of being the base sanitation inspector. Meaning that I would inspect all food service areas, food delivery trucks, clubs, canteens, commissary, barber shops, swimming pools, coffee messes, etc. I could just about stick my nose into any situation that I could justify as a health hazard.

I was provided with a Navy pick up truck and each morning I would depart the dispensary with a flash light, clip board and a list of several places I had scheduled to inspect. Later in the day I would return to type reports on the sanitary conditions in each establishment and submit them to the Officer in Charge. Part of my duties also included training and the issue of food service cards to new hirers.' Holding cursory screening physicals on personnel attending cooking school and personnel serving brig time.

I also correlated venereal disease contacts with state and city officials. It was a very sad state of affairs when a married sailor contracted Gonorrhea and lived in Navy Housing. He was giving the order to go home, tell his wife of his medical condition and within twenty-four hours bring her in for examination and if positive investigate her possible contacts. He would be intensely interviewed to his extra marital contacts. In some cases, the spouse would contract the disease from his wife. The excuse I heard the most was, "he was gone too long." If the wife did not report then I would have the task of speaking to her directly.

Gonorrhea is a sexually transmitted disease. It can cause infections in the genitals, rectum and throat. It cannot be caught off a toilet seat, unless it's the place you had sex. I remember one officer's school close to the dispensary had a very sexually active Wave working there. The count was around nineteen people both staff and students that she infected with gonorrhea. Take those nineteen individuals plus their sexual partners plus their contacts takes one hell of an effort to get everyone treated. It has been said that only the drips get the drip.

I started my new assignment like a house afire. It didn't take me long to understand the Dave syndrome back in San Jose. Once I walked into an establishment, it was all smiles. Women workers rushed to put their hairnets on; cover exposed food in the reefers, while others were swabbing decks showing me that they were on the stick.

The manager or the person in charge had a line of bullshit for every discrepancy I pointed out. The more I wrote, the more worry began showing on the workers faces. I was young and had no concept of worker's job security.

To justify my report, one or two workers would be blamed for the sanitary violations and terminated. That made it Hunky-dory. We supposedly now had a facility with no problems.

I learned a crucial lesson the day I inspected the Chief Petty Officer's Club. It was a going place and located off the base just outside gate four. Retired Chief, Don Bonneville was the manager. (A sailor came to Newport) Pat Brady was his assistant. (A Sailor Came to Newport) Eventually the club would move into a new building inside base and Bonneville would follow. However, this particular day in the old club things were not good. As I kept writing violations the more excitable Bonneville became. The inspection found the sanitary conditions of the club to be unacceptable.

I informed Mr. Bonneville to close the club and get it cleaned up for a follow up inspection in the morning. If he resisted then, I would have no recourse than to notify the Commanding Officer.

The truth of the matter was that in no way did I have the authority to contact the Commanding Officer. Nobody else but me knew that and when I used it I always got results.

When I returned to the dispensary Chief Perry was waiting for me. Motioning me to sit down in the chair beside his desk, he didn't waste words.

"Have you gone out of your fucking mind?"

The statement took me by surprise I honestly didn't know what he was talking about.

"You can sit there with a blank look on your face but you are about to have every Chief on this base after your ass. They will make your life aboard this base miserable. You my friend have stepped into a world of shit."

No way doing my job did I think it would end up with mass retaliation? It was my turn to squirm. I knew it was a bad move to piss off a Chief but all of them!

"What do you want me to do Chief? I haven't handed in the report."

Leaning in close the Chief's voice was almost at a whisper.

"Get in your truck, go back to the Club, and tell Bonneville your not going to submit your report. If he gets the place cleaned up in a hurry then he can stay open. I'm not telling you to forget your job; I'm saying there is more than one way to skin a cat. You got him shook up; he'll bring people in and clean the place up. You will have accomplished your job.

I followed the Chiefs advice. The club did get cleaned up, and I developed a much better working relationship with Don Bonneville. I did realize that he must have called Chief Perry. The Navy operates on the knowledge and experience of its Chiefs. I was thankful for Chief Perry's advice.

As time went on I acquired maturity in my inspections. It was not that I could put your ass in a sling but rather working together we can get the job done.

Wilfred Magnum was retired Army. (A Dog Face Came to Newport) Wilfred was the food service manger at the Officer's Club. Wilfred was always under the gun. Just about the time he had it all together they would hit him with several social events, shrimp-a-peal, all the fish you can eat, retirement parties, birthdays, the list goes on.

Wilfred had to produce with a crew of minimum wage workers. Most lasted a few days and never showed up again. Wilfred would run around the kitchen doing the jobs that he had no help for. His job was not easy.

His boss and manager of the club was Donald Booth. (A Sailor Came to Newport) During numerous inspections of the Officurs club I never met him. His responsibility seems to focus on the clubs agenda and catering to high-ranking officers. There were many times I thought Wilfred would throw in the towel, but he always hung in there. He was a man to be admired.

The Navy Exchange was another horse of a different color. They ran the base cafeterias, canteen trucks, and bowling alleys. Their primary goal was to make a profit, and everything else was secondary. My first inspection was in a building where sandwiches were being prepared for sale. Regulations called that a prepared sandwich could not be sold after forty-eight hours. After that they were to be disposed as garbage. This was accomplished by placing color-coded tape on each sandwich. Lets say the sandwiches made on Monday would all have a strip of red tape affixed to the sandwich wrap. Come Wednesday and not being sold they would be discarded as trash. Did it take a rocket scientist to know all that had to be done to extend the life of the sandwich was to change the color of the tape? The sandwich was place in a light cardboard holder then wrapped with cellophane wrap. I recommended the tapes to be placed on the holder so it couldn't be removed without opening the sandwich. Great idea! But it got me nowhere. My first lesson in politics above the enlisted level.

Gene Harvey was the Navy Exchanges main boss of food service. At first he thought me a pain in the ass but later on that relationship improved considerably. He had a good-looking secretary; her first name was Ann, she was a lady's ladies', super person. I wonder why men in a position of authority all have good-looking secretaries.

Gene also had a boat where he would entertain policy makers of the base. When I had to go up against one of these people it was like hitting my head against the wall, especially when my boss was one of his guests. I would get the word, "I'll take care of it," and that would be it.

Mr. Rodgers was the manager of the snack bar located in the Library on Coasters Island. (A Sailor Came to Newport) When I walked in he would start worrying. I don't know why as he ran a clean operation. We came to be good friends. I greatly valued his opinions and advise.

The barbershops were something else. I had to check disinfectant solutions, the general cleanliness and that the barbers were indeed sanitizing their instruments. It was pretty routine except for the shop at Officers Candidate School. It was a busy place having five to six barbers.

The barber in charge was a guy named Mo. He was a big time operator, and the truth is I didn't want to know his extra curricular activities. He had a back room where he would disappear with various people. I could have entered, but the shop was up to standards and the backroom had nothing to do with it, so I skipped it. Knowing Mo it probably was a smart move. I surmised that it had to do with cigarettes.

At the main exchange barbershop there were four barbers, all experienced and professional. I would talk to them all, but I always ended up talking to a barber they called Don. Years later I would find his barber shop in Tiverton. He had a nice business with a huge following. When I walked in we had a good laugh, he wanted to know if I was going to hold an inspection? Don was so well liked that when you walked into his shop there would be twelve guys in front of you. Nobody ever left; you sat down shot the bull and waited your turn. It was tragic and sad day when I learned that Don had succumbed to cancer.

There were two mess halls on the base that were operated by Naval foodservice personnel. One galley ran with contracted civilian workers. They were under the direction of Chief Duffy. Now let me tell you, he could be one mean Stew Burner. He was a big dude and as mean as they came. Nobody in that galley wanted Duffy on his or her ass. Consequently, the place was spotless. **(A Sailor came to Newport)**

One of my inspection stations that very few knew about was located at the Melville

129

Basin. I would drive down to Melville on a weekly basis to inspect the Small Craft tied up there and a concrete building housing a barracks on one side and cooking school in the opposite side. Just before I turned on Burma Road to return to the base, I would take a sharp right onto a dirt road that led me to the sewage treatment plant! Two civilian operators ran the plant. Both were certified sewage plant operators; there was not much for me to inspect. At certain times, they would spread the sludge out on the grounds behind the plant. There is one plant life that survives and goes with the sludge. That seed is the tomato. The plants grow rapidly out of the sludge. It is quite a sight to see a field of tomatoes plants with bunches of bright red fruit and no pickers.

Chapter 29

All in all, I settled into a daily routine. I knew just about everybody and everybody knew me. I learned to deal with the smiles and waves when I entered to hold an inspection and the finger to my back when I left.

Each morning an old Volkswagen Bus would pull up to the front of the dispensary. It would be loaded down with ice covered whole chickens. It was one of the few vendors that the commissary bought directly off.

Consequently, I had to inspect every delivery to approve its acceptance.

The company went by the name of "IDEAL" located on Long Wharf, off Marlborough Street. The delivery driver was one heck of a nice guy. He was a retired Newport Police Officer, and I guess his last name was Pine. There was never a time that I ever had to refuse his deliveries because of a sanitation problem.

One particular night I left the Petty Officers Club at Gate Two. I turned left onto Connell Highway, then bounced off the railroad tracks, cleared the curbing, and came to a halt in the middle of the rotary circle. The right-hand tire had blown leaving a deep rut across the grassy surface. I did what any Sailor would do. I got out of the car and took off.

I walked home to Mahan Street, explaining to my wife I had a flat I couldn't fix. I would have to have it taken care of in the morning.

Of course, I had to walk to work in the morning. I was inspecting the chicken truck and mentioned the trouble I was in. When I finished telling him my story, he grinned and told me to settle down he would take care of it. He emphasized that I would not have a car for at least a week. I went home and broke that news to my wife.

The next morning during Ideals inspection I was informed that my car was in the back of a garage on West Broadway. It would have to sit there for three or four days. It was a precaution in case the State was looking for a car that caused the damage to the traffic circle.

After the cooling off period, they put a used tire back on my car so it wouldn't have a new look. I was thankful the day I picked up my car. I owed a bill for towing, a bill for a used tire and a voluntary payment for a hundred dollars for what the garage crew called beer money. I gladly complied.

Things were a little uptight at my residence, but everything went off just like he said. The man saved my young ass from big trouble. We would run into each other years later when he was working at Salve.

Chapter 30

Working at the dispensary I met and became close friends with Cliff Chase. (A **Sailor From Newport**)

Cliff could not believe that I knew nothing about salt-water fishing. It ended up with us going to Ames in Middletown where I purchased a casting rod, reel, line, sinkers and whatever Cliff pointed out that I would need. From there it was back to the dispensary

132

where we put a complete casting rig together. From there, we went over to Mahon Street where my wife had made us both "Salmon Pea Wiggle." Cliff had never heard of it, but he scoffed it down like it was going out of style.

After supper, we helped clean up and left for the bait shop before it closed. We purchased a dozen green crabs. I had never seen one before and wasn't too impressed. First it was a stop at McGee's for a couple of beer. Cliff, I swear knew everybody. As the evening started to settle in, Cliff had McGee put six cold ones in a bag, and we left.

I had been out around Ocean Drive a couple of times with the family, but I was not r familiar with it. We parked off the road, and I thought we were somewhere close to the halfway mark. Rock jetties extended out into the water, and the surge of the surf made it rough. It didn't take long, and I was soaked from the waist down.

I received a quick lesson from Cliff on how to cut a green crab in half, attach the hook through its legs and then cast it out into the sea. A year went by, and I never caught a fish, but I drowned a whole slew of green crabs.

This is one of my Cliff Chase sea stories. We were down in Blood Alley, and Cliff was feeling no pain. I don't recall just what he did, but he grabbed me by the shirtsleeve, telling me to run. We ran along the waterfront with both the police and Shore Patrol chasing us. I think we were down, near the Parascandolus pier. Cliff pulled me down and we belly crawled under a truck. The police had a dog, and it wasn't too friendly.

He was growling at us, and we were staring at him. Cliff was always one to take charge. His suggestion, "we give our selves up." It was my first and last trip to the holding cells at gate ten.

Soon after Cliff received orders to Vietnam. I never saw too much of him again. The story that I was told was that Cliff developed a type of fatal cancer. Knowing that, he went to the O'Neil's Funeral Parlor on Spring Street and tried out caskets until he found the one he felt the most comfortable in.

Chapter 31

My wife announced the good news that she was pregnant. Thus far family living had gone been pretty well, but Mahon Street was starting to change. The days of Sam Dawley riding herd over the association's rules and regulations were noticeably absent.

I could tell by the trash cans that were being left in the street. People were moving in had no jobs and could care less about getting one. They would party half the night when waiting for the doors to open that distributed their welfare checks and food stamps. The checks were to aid families that were down and out. On Mahan Street, it went mostly for cigarettes, booze and dope.

I started looking at a possible move. Nothing was cheap in Newport, and I was certainly the low man on the totem pole. I can't remember just how it came about, but I stopped in at "Colonial Real estate," on West Main Road. I met the most humorous guy of my life. He had a smile that wouldn't quit; there was no doubt in my mind that he was one hundred percent Irish! With a name like Francis Dwyer could there be any doubt?

Frank was unbelievable helpful in my quest to rent or buy a house. We went over my personal income, savings and debts. Relating to my present position his personal advice was for me was to buy a five-man tent. Seeing the look on my face, he cracked up laughing. Giving me his big grin he patted me on the shoulder telling me the office manager had encouraging news. I couldn't help but ask if he was going to give me the location of some good tent sales. This time we both cracked up.

Bill Beltz was the manager of Colonial Real Estate. He was a retired Navy Warrant Officer. (A Sailor Came to Newport)

135

All three of us sat around a desk with Bill jotting down notes on a lined tablet. They explained that President Johnson had signed a bill to help active duty personnel purchase homes. It was an In Service FHA loan requiring no money down.

Before I got too excited, Bill explained that the mandate for the loan was complicated. Not for commissioned officers but not so easy for white hats. I would be required to have the cash for the closing costs up front. It would have to be in a savings account, and it could not be borrowed.

Frank spread out a bank chart that gave the bank requirements, based on the cost of the house and the salary of the buyer. I did not meet the requirements. I felt my bubble burst.

They gave me a few minutes while Bill flipped the pages on his pad and pushed it across the table to Frank.

"Life is never easy, if you're ready to buy a house, Frank will start the ball rolling. The paper work could take a month or longer, but your will to succeed starts now."

Standing, Bill put his hand out to me. Taking it, he had the last word of advise. I am leaving you in good hands, just beware of the Leprechauns. They usually pick your pockets while Frank is talking to them.

Walking Bill to the door, Frank returned to the desk with a sheepish Irish grin. He pushed Bills pencil and a pad toward me.

"You might want to take a few notes. The first and most important issue is raising the money for the closing costs. That done then the FHA will guarantee your bank loan. I would estimate a down payment of fifteen hundred dollars. You will have to pay property tax and property insurance for a year in advance and have no credit card debts."

Frank knew how I must have been feeling as he gave me one of his big grins.

"Other people in your position have borrowed from their parents, sold valuables, cashed bonds, used a re-enlisted bonus and did what ever else it took to raise money. Of course, the most immediate way is to get a second job."

Standing Frank assured me that the ball was in my court and that all things including buying a house were possible. We shook hands and called it a day. He gave me his phone number and told me when I had a plan of action to call.

Chapter 32

With the coming addition of another child, I knew that time had come to get out of the project. I wanted a place that my family could call home. Frank had suggested the possibility of a re-enlistment bonus. I was eligible and made arrangements to ship over. When that day came, we would add the amount of the bonus to our savings account.

I answered an ad for a morning janitor at the Moose Lodge on Connell Highway. I got the job, so seven days a week I was there at six a.m. to do my thing.

I had a good friend Dan Gleason, (A Sailor Came to Newport) He was retired and nightly he had the job of topping off the beer machines in the base bowling alleys. He wanted some time off, so I started filling in three times a week. Can you believe five different brands of beer in each machine, for twenty-five cents a can?

The Petty Officers Club at Gate two, served lunch. The manager, Jerry Sawtell (A Sailor Came to Newport) needed a short order cook during the noon hour. I started that day.

Mean while I heard of a job requiring a janitor to clean the Field House at Gate 17 on Sunday Mornings. I was hired. The field house housed a cafeteria. At night, Big Pete ran the place. (A Sailor Came to Newport) I just can't remember his last name. We were on the Grand Canyon together, and when he retired, he went to work for JT O'Connell in the lumber section. He spotted me one Sunday and offered me a job cooking two or three nights a week. I took it. I now was on Jean Harvey's payroll. So what? I needed to buy a house.

The night job at the Field house required a little bit of shifting around as I had applied and been accepted at Grants Department store on Connell Highway. I worked in the Hardware Department with Tony Mastrocinque. **(A Sailor came to Newport)** He also served on the Grand Canyon. The guy running the auto department I believe his last name was Kinsella, always wore a blue suit and flew airplanes. Eddie Reposa worked in the garage; he never refused a cold one. I have to mention another employee, Dorothy Connell. Everybody loved her. The only woman I ever knew that always gave her husband a single red rose and served him breakfast in bed. Lucky Bastard.

I met the guidelines for an FHA loan, so Frank started showing me properties. I found my house in the area of Broadway, across from the Jesus Savior Church. I don't want to identify the property, as it is still active.

The house was in bad shape, bad, but the potential was there. The price was $9,300.00. I went for it. Frank made arrangements to finalize the deal, and set up a closing date. It all went remarkably smooth. I had a gang from the dispensary that helped me move.

139

A phone call informed me my wife was in the hospital. I had to stop and head for the maturity ward. The gang kept on moving, and one of the wives took care of the girls. The house was inhabitable; every room was a mess, the kitchen unbelievable. After our belongings had been moved, more wives were called in. With buckets, detergents, disinfectants and rags they tackled the down stairs bedroom. They scrubbed it from the top to bottom. It smelled like a hospital laboratory. Next was the kitchen that would be a mammoth task.

Our bed and the girl's twin beds were moved into the scrubbed out bedroom. It would be crowded but it was clean and ready for the arrival of the little one. Our belongings had all been moved to the inside of the house.

Cliff my old friend came over to help with the cleaning. With him looking after the girls, I was able to be at the hospital for the birth of a son. Two days later Cliff watched over the girls, plus working his tail off scrubbing chewing tobacco juice that had been spit on the living room wall. His helping out enabled me to go to the hospital and bring home the newest member of the family. Our new son went straight into what we referred to as the sterile room! There was a lot of work to be done, but it didn't matter, it was our home.

A short time later Cliff got his orders for the Fleet Marine Force in Vietnam. He was a close friend. He came for supper, said goodbye and left. We all missed him.

I continued my other jobs as the expense of fixing the house up was mounting. We would go up to Kerr mill in Fall River and buy six rolls of wallpaper for ten bucks. We were wallpapering fools. I had used up about all my acquired leave shortly after buying the house. In a way, it kept us home and busy. We were a real family.

The day of the official closing seven of us met at Colonial Real Estate. Bill, Frank, and the Lawyer representing the sellers. Also present was Mr. and Mrs. Larry Settle. (A Sailor Came to Newport) They too were there to close on a house. The process went smoothly and before we knew it; the four of us were homeowners. Bill and Frank brought the four of us to the Officers Club on the Naval Base. We were served a great meal at their expense. Over the years when Larry and I would meet we would reminisce about our first real estate deals.

It was in July of 1966 when I received my orders to report to Camp Lejeune, North Carolina for Marine training, for further transfer to the 3rd Marine Division, Vietnam.

On a personal note, at the same time my mother was a patient at the Hanover Hospital in Hanover, New Hampshire. Her prognosis was poor. Cancer had spread through most of her body. The Doctor's pronouncement was not good, a month, maybe.

I was the only son, my father was deceased and I thought as the only heir, the only child, I might get my orders delayed for ninety days. I put in a special request chit to my commanding officer. It was refused.

Leaving was not easy, like the many husbands that had gone to Vietnam before me I could only hold my wife and children close, give them a hug and kiss and leave.

It would have made a lot more sense if I had known, that our South Vietnamese ally, Major General Nguyen Ky, would some day open a liquor store in California.

Chapter 33

Picture this! The last time I got off the bus in my whites tugging on to a sea bag was in front of the Newport YMCA. Now I find myself getting off the bus again, dressed in my whites and dragging my sea bag behind me. The difference is this time I am in Jacksonville, North Carolina. It is the home of Camp Lejeune, one of the largest Marine bases on the East Coast. If I ever felt intimidated it was then. Standing there in my sailor suit surrounded by at least three hundred Marines. I thought I was about to get my ass kicked.

"Hey Doc, checking in to Field Med School?

The voice came from a Marine sitting in a pickup truck.

I nodded affirmably.

"Throw your bag in the back of the truck and get in, you're the third squid to check in today."

My first reaction was to call him a dumb ass Jar Head. I thought better of it and maintained my silence by checking out the local sites. I couldn't get over how green everything was.

The grunt dropped me off in front of the building telling me that it was where I was to check in. He just had to pull my chain once more.

"Is that beanie on your head called a squid hat?"

Retrieving my sea bag, I stood along side the drivers door.

"Say Marine, do you even know why the Navy Department established the Marine Corps?"

He mentioned something about Congress, but it made little sense.

143

Lifting my sea bag to my shoulder, I gave him the answer.

"It was to give the Sailors someone to dance with."

I was surprised as hell when he cracked up laughing.

"That was a good one Doc, Semper Fi."

Things went a long rather smoothly. The First sergeant had me check in, took my records and then led me back the supply room. Here I would be given a set of Marine utilities; boots, belt and a hat. I was also given a cardboard container to fold neatly and store away anything Navy. The purpose? Outside of the building was an archway that you passed under to enter the main compound. The archway was inscribed with a quote that read similar following to the following.

"Through this archway walk the best Doc's in the world."

Under that was the name, "Chesty Puller." I have been unable to verify the quote. All I can remember is a few words related to it. The First Sergeant explained the formalities.

"You did not walk under the arch with your Navy uniform on, but dressed in your new Marine green utilities; you're a Marine!

Jim Mullins, (A Sailor came to Newport) and Francis Flynn, (A Sailor came to Newport) also

144

arrived from Newport. So I did have someone from Newport to talk to. Francis hadn't changed since our days in MEMQ. He was plastered all the time, and when he came to Lejeune, he brought his sixty-seven year old girl friend with him. That was not too much of a problem as they were living in a motel off base. However, Sunday rolled around, and they showed up at the chapel for mass. Francis was juiced. The priest was giving his sermon when the girl friend stumbled into the main isle and started shouting at the priest to let Francis stay home, she didn't want her poor Francis to go to any dumb ass war. Ushers came and took them out of the church. Francis didn't have a clue to what was going on.

I had a few observations concerning our training. Not being in too good of shape I noticed that the Marine Instructors could do fifty push ups with one hand, five hundred jumping jacks, and with a full combat pack on their backs run five miles without stopping, they had no necks.

Their DI hats appeared to sit on their shoulders. When they spoke, it was like a deep growl coming up from their stomachs.

"You are the most pathetic bunch of squids that ever set foot in front of me. You are fat and lazy typical Navy sailors. Fall In!"

145

Falling into ranks we were marched to a Quonset hut and herded inside. It was simple enough. The gas would come, and we would sing the Marine Corps Hymn.

Ten minutes later we were outside lying on the ground puking our guts out. I swear I saw no neck grin when he assured us it would get better as we went along.

I was on my back laying half dirt, and half mud crawling under barbed wire, which was just above my head. I had a rifle that I was holding on my chest. Using that I would lift the wire and move forward by pushing with the heels of my boots. There were explosions going on all around me with the addition of live machine gun rounds being fired over my head. I kept repeating the warning I heard when I left the trench, "don't standup."

Our orders were that we would be transported directly to Vietnam from Camp Lejeune and there would be no in between leave. There were three other guys from the Rhode Island area and Jim and me from Newport.

We rented a vehicle and on a Friday when liberty call went we headed north. Way out of bounds and if we asked the trip would have never been approved. We all reasoned like Marines. "What are they going to do? Send us to Vietnam?

146

I spent nine hours with my family; it was so worth the trip. My wife and the girls kept making fun of my new haircut. Once again, I held my son kissed the girls and my wife goodbye then left.

Chapter 34

Jim and I both had orders to report to Da Nang. He was assigned to the Military Police Company with the First Marine Division. I went to the Medical Battalion, Third Marine Division.

I saw Jim every once in a while. His compound was some distance away. I was starting my third week in country when the Battalion Master Chief notified me to pack up I was going north. Being the newest man to check in and shit does run down hill I wasn't surprised.

I had been working with a third class that the Master Chief was thinking about sending up north with me. He was a young corpsman from upstate New York. His squad was out in the bush, pooping and snooping for signs of the enemy.

The squad not knowing, walked into a minefield, and he was the only one to walk out. He should have been sent home. He did not want to go north, and I was thankful when the Master Chief decided not to send him. The kid was messed up, and it didn't take a brain surgeon to see it. He had me wound up tight.

I climbed onto the back of a Marine six-by and made myself a seat on the floor. We were part of a motorized convoy of thirty or so various Marine trucks. The Marines in the back of the six-by were referred to as Rough Riders. For any reason, the convoy came to a stop, they would bail off the truck, with me in tow. Perimeters were established along both sides of convoy. They varied in distance giving little chance for the enemy to surprise us.

When the convoy stopped, and we were in the middle of a village they would stand in line and move forward. If the villagers resisted,, then they would fire well over their heads, forcing them back and away. I got off a few rounds myself. The kids would be begging for handouts, but it was "Dee Dee." Meaning get the hell out of here! It would not be unusual for a kid to stuff a grenade down a trucks fuel pipe.

Most of the time there were two or three Huey's constantly flying above us. I broke the ice with a few of the Marines, but they were a hostile bunch. I would soon learn why. I felt better when they started calling me "Doc." When they stated talking about the Marine Corps, it was always referred to as the "Crotch."

One of the grunts broke out a case of C-rats and threw me a Ham and Lima Beans. I could tell from the word go, they were waiting to see my reaction when I chowed down. The reaction was great. It it was the first time I heard any of them laugh.

Ham and Lima Beans without a doubt was the worse can of crap I had ever eaten in my life. I got several words of encouragement while I watched them chow down like we were at McDonalds.

Finishing had them mostly sitting around bitching about the crotch. They got into a serious discussion and what I could hear from the back of the truck they were trying to determine who was going to take the Lieutenant out. They were about to draw straws when we pulled into Phu Bai.

We would spend the night, stay with the vehicles and leave at daybreak for Dong Ha. The Marines set up a perimeter watch.

The next morning I was assigned to drive a lightweight truck to Dong Ha. It was filled with medical gear, insecticide and parts to a fogging machine. The word I got was that the Engineers at Dong Ha, would turn it into a fogging machine to be used to spray mosquitos. The amount of Malaria cases was increasing markedly with most infected men being sent to the Hospital Ship off the coast of Da Nang.

The rough riders had already moved toward the front of the Convoy. For the first time, I was able to count five Rough Rider trucks. I was directed to pull in-between another small truck and a jeep.

We passed by Hue and continued up Route nine to Quang Tri, then north to Dong Ha. It was the first convoy to make the trip from Da Nang to Dong Ha with out casualties. The word was that soon we would be in support of Operation Hastings.

Dong Ha was a wonderful place. There was a runway where C-123's and C-130's could land, go to the end of the runway, hurling everything out the back of the aircraft. This included Marines getting off and Marines trying to get on. A fast spin of the tail section put the plane heading back down the runway and taking off. Stopping was out of the question.

Dong Ha was a forward Marine firebase with plans to increase its size into a much larger base. I heard from the rumor machine that the build up of Dong Ha, Camp Carroll, Rock Pile, Khe Sanh, Con Thien, etc. was in support of construction of the separation barrier between North and South Vietnam. I believe this was the brainchild of Robert McNamara, who was then the Secretary of Defense.

As time passed, and not wanting to spend pages on detail, I came to one conclusion. Robert had a good plan, well thought out. He had half the Marine Corps, Navy Sea Bees, Air Force, Army tanks, all ready to go. Robert must have been thinking that if he kicked a little ass, the wall could be completed in a month's time. Robert had all of his Tee's crossed, but his major downfall was he didn't get permission from Ho Chi Minh.

Chapter 35

War sucks. Dong Ha sucks, death sucks, the crotch sucks, the chow sucks, Grave Registration sucks, the Monsoons suck, sleeping on the ground sucks, sharing your rubber lady with a rat the size of a cat sucks, all in all it would be very difficult to find something here at Dong Ha that didn't suck.

Graves Registration is where Marines that have been killed are cleaned up; body parts accounted for, and then sent on to Da Nang. That is a pretty big place, and I'm not sure just what they do. When they are finished, the body is put in an airtight metal shipping container. Stacked up on pallets; a forklift loads them aboard an aircraft for their trip home.

When I arrived in Dong Ha, Graves Registration had no refrigeration. Body bags were lying in the sun. They were so swollen I thought they were going to burst. The flies and maggots were unbelievable. There were two pump sprayers on the truck I had driven up from Phu Bia. I took one and filled it with insecticide, then sprayed the hell out of the whole area. Walking beside the swollen bags, I couldn't help but wonder who was inside? How they bought the ranch? And where was there hometown?

Graves Registration also acted as an unofficial supply depot. I found a pair of boots that were my size, a flax jacket with a few bloodstains across the front and a helmet, with ink markings written on its cloth cover. Most of the inscriptions were written inside drawn hearts. Maybe his girlfriend maybe his wife but he seemed to keep his sanity by continually writing heart messages. I wore the helmet for the next twelve months. There were no identities to who he was, but the name of a girl was the main subject of every heart.

When I turned my gear in, I brought the heart messages to the attention of the sergeant working there. He read them then took the cloth liner off the helmet.

"Doc I know where you're coming from but even if I could make contact with the people he wrote about, which I see as nearly impossible, a lot of time has gone by. Maybe she re-married, would this be a good thing? Tell you what, leave it, I'll do what I can."

That sounded good to me. "Semper Fi."

Life at Dong Ha wasn't too bad for a crap hole. It was the rainy season, and it never stopped. Mixing in with the ground dirt it produced a field of mud. Your boots would sink in four or five inches into the mud. When you lifted your boot up, you would get a swishing noise. The Grunts referred to it as Mud Fucking.

The roads they had were laden with mud holes. Even if I could find the Engineers and they built a sprayer on the back of the truck, the weight would sink it to the axels. I was able to bunk in with three Marines in a bombed out building that the French Foreign Legion had left. The Marines made up the motor pool. There was no roof, but the Marines had secured a shelter half over the building that kept most of the rain out. I had enough room so I could move the gear off the truck and keep it dry.

Whoever loaded the truck had tossed in three rubber ladies. They were no more than an air mattress designed to give you some comfort when sleeping on the ground. I had no trouble trading a couple to the Marines for a case of C-rations.

I was beat and wasted no time putting my rubber lady to use. I was in a deep sleep when I could hear some movement near me. Turning on my flashlight, I was looking eye to eye with one big ass rat. He didn't move it was like he wanted to know who in hell gave me permission to move in.

I would set out wire cages at night using peanut butter from our C-rations for bait. When inside the wire spring-loaded door would close, and the rat was trapped. Some were so big they would push the door back open and getaway.

There is a danger of flea's leaving the rat and spreading their disease. The Marines in the motor pool were able to get me a fifty-five-gallon barrel that we filled with water. Anytime we caught a rat we dropped the rat and the cage into the barrel. Next morning we would pull the cages out, bury the rats and start a new day.

It didn't take long for someone to come up with the idea to trap a mongoose. The reason being that a mongoose supposedly has the fastest metabolic rate of any other animal in the world. I was told if they didn't eat or drink constantly they would die. Live traps were set; a screened cage was constructed, and we waited.

It was unbelievable how it came together. The two combatants, the mongoose and the biggest rat we could capture, were put in a cage. It was covered over with canvas and bets were made to who would be the winner. The next morning the canvas would be removed to reveal the champion. Interest began to wean. Two rats, a bat, and a snake fell to the onslaught of the mighty mongoose. A proven warrior he was set free.

A Chief Corpsman had been sent up from Da Dang to take charge of Preventive Medicine issues in the I Corps area. Not a bad idea but the Master Chief in Da Nang had no clue that the Monsoon was upon us and nobody was going nowhere. The Chief seemed to be a pretty solid guy. He was from someplace in the Carolina's. He wrote long letters every day to which he referred to as his sweetheart. He confided in us, that he was married but that a divorce was in the making. On the other hand, he was planning to marry his sweetheart who was just turning sixteen.

The Chief hadn't been at Dong Ha a month when he got his "Dear John" letter. He turned into a lovesick maniac. If only he had a phone, he could call. He blamed the letter on his wife who he said did not get along with his little sweetheart. He saw the Chaplin in an effort to get emergency leave. He was turned down.

I couldn't remember where I had been; I'm thinking Camp Carroll. I knew that I was tired and beat. When I entered the shack, I dropped my junk in a pile and collapsed on my rubber lady. I had noticed the Chief sitting on an ammo box but I hadn't paid much attention.

I heard the sound of a slide being pulled back on the barrel of a forty-five. The next sound I heard was a gunshot. Having no idea what he was doing I crawled on my knees out the door and into the mud. The result was that the Chief shot himself in the foot and yes he was on his way home.

During the investigation the First Sergeant in filling out his report, measured the projectile of the round once it left his foot. It hit the wall in three places and spent out on my rubber lady.

When the investigation was over The First Sergeant presented me with the slug,

"Doc, this is the closest you will ever come and know it."

I still have the slug.

Chapter 36

Dong Ha continued to build up. We would get hit with a few rounds at night but so far they had stayed away from the wire.

One particular morning I was walking through the officer's compound when a civilian wished me a good morning. I was surprised as civilians were restricted from coming this far north. Very unusual, but I figured he was here as part of McNamara's DMZ plan.

I told him he sounded like a Red Neck! He countered by saying I sounded like a Vermont Yankee. I told him that he was close that I was a New Hampshire Yankee. He told me that he had several friends that lived in New Hampshire. He visited often, but his home was in Rhode Island. He followed that up asking me if I ever heard of Newport? I asked him if he ever the name of the street I lived on? The two of us stood there trying to grasp the reality that were standing in the Northern Province of South Vietnam, mud up to our ass and lived less than a mile apart in Newport.

His name was, Harold (Zeke) St. John. (A Sailor Came to Newport) I asked him what was going on with the DMZ. I could tell he was not about to discuss it. I mentioned that we heard from the grunts that as fast, and we put up a watchtower the NVA would blow it. If Zeke knew anything, he wasn't saying.

The shelling of Dong Ha by the NVA began to pick up. Most of the rounds were Russian Rockets and did a lot of damage. They ordered Zeke back to the rear. I dug my hole deeper.

For reasons that I just can't remember, I accompanied a Marine Warrant Officer through the village of Dong Ha to a Catholic Church, located just west of the village. The Warrant mentioned that he was from

Woonsocket, Rhode Island. He was surprised when I told him I was from Newport.

From the looks of the church it must have been built during the French occupation. The Priest met us as we approached the front steps. Shaking the Warrants hand, he led us around the side of the church to the entranceway to his small office. Once in side he clasped my hand and gave me a chair to sit down.

I had seen him out riding his motorbike from village to village. I would always think to myself that he was very chancy with the Viet Cong not being too keen on the Catholic religion.

He would be at one end of the village, and a Buddhist Monk dressed in his orange robes would be at the other end. Monks carried begging pots under their robes to collect food scraps from the villagers' the handouts on the part of the villagers was mandatory not voluntary.

Just outside each village there would be a structure made from whatever material was available. Most were made out of rolled sheet metal and resembled the size of a telephone booth.

Having a door on one side, the Monk was able to step inside close the door and dial up Buda directly. I'll never tell who slammed a length of pipe against the outside wall. The door flew open, and the Monks orange color robe had change from orange to brown.

Sorry, I got side tracked. We're going back inside the Priest office where the Priest just poured us a small amount of brandy. Picking up on the conversation, I believe that the Warrant was involved in a people to people program. He would pass donations from the states to the Priest for a nearby orphanage.

With the talks over, the priest invited us to stay and attend mass. The inside of the church was well kept. The alter was adorned with religious items and covered with a rich satin fabric. I was surprised at the number of Viennese that attended.

At the end of the mass, we said our goodbyes to the priest, his alter boys, and left.

Not long after we had attended mass the Viet Cong stormed the church killing the Priest, and the two alter boys. They left their mark by blowing up the church.

Chapter 37

The day finely came when I could put the three hundred and sixty-fifth X mark on my short timers calendar. I'm going home!

A United 707 aircraft landed in Da Nang carrying a full load of fresh troops. It would turn around and leave with a full load of survivors.

As I took my seat, I knew that I shared one common thought with my fellow passengers.

"Let's get this big mother fucker off the ground."

The plane was quickly filling up, yet we sat in silence. We all met and knew the enemy well enough to know that we were still in harms way. There is no sensible way to be thinking of home when the brain keeps sending impulses of immediate destruction.

A Marine took a seat beside me. He said nothing. For no particular reason I tried to remember the words to;

"Be the first one on your block to have your kid come home in a box."

I tried making myself calm down. My imagination had Jane Fonda at the end of the runway standing on top of an NVA tank waiting to take us out. She was grinning.

The engines began to roar, as the plane taxied for takeoff. I took one last look out the window as the plane roared forward. I prayed that I would never have to return to this pile of shit again. The noise from the jet engines abated as the plane began its climb into the wild blue yonder.

The tension that gripped every passenger on take off instantly faded away when a fairly attractive stewardess made her way down the aisle. A voice from the mid section of the plane bellowed out loud and clear.

"It's a round eye; It's a round eye!"

That was followed up with several more chants of, "It's a round eye," "It's a round eye," It's a round eye."

The voice of the Captain sounded out over the planes intercom system.

"Just thought you would like to know that we have left the Vietnam air space."

That brought everyone to cheer. There were handshakes, tears, dancing in the isle as the realization of going home was now a reality.

Tired almost to the point of psychological exhaustion, I leaned back in my seat. A multitude of memories were all vying to be number one in my priority of thinking. The subconscious over ruled, and I sat there thinking about my relief. His name was Liles.

The first night he reported he took a couple hunks of shrapnel in his back. A few nights later he got hit again. Two purple hearts and you were shipped back to rear with the gear. Before he could get transferred he received wounds for the third time. Three Purple Hearts and you were shipped out of country. The Irony was that he beat me home.

He was on a plane ahead of mine. At least he wasn't in a body bag.

Several years later we would meet again and over a few beers we both wondered who took his place.

Chapter 38

"Newport!" I made it home. I'm safe. I'm with my family. The Vietnam experience is just a bad memory that will soon go away. So I thought.

When I could finally accept that it was safe to leave the house, I made my first venture to Ocean Drive. I stood on the side of the road looking down on the waves splashing over the rocks. I thought of the nights that Cliff Chase and myself would sit out here half the night drinking beer trying to catch a Black Fish. I watched in awe as the incoming waves slammed against the ledge of rocks. The force of the water created a shower of white caps shooting high above the rocks.

I asked myself a question. How could I be living in a poncho, nonstop rain, mud up to my ass, trying to eat a can of ham and lima beans? Then like a magician's illusion, I'm standing in the sun looking at one of the most stunning views on the planet.

It was a great feeling to be welcomed home. People would ask me what it was like over there? My answer was always the same.

"Imagine yourself running through rice patties, water up to your knees, toting sixty-five pounds of gear strapped to your back. The water is splashing all around you, when you realize it's not raining!"

A very special neighbor was Margret Warner. While raising her family, she took the time to ensure that my family was always cared for. Being a widow, she supported her family plus having to endure the pain from the loss of a son, who had just entered the Priest hood.

Of course, who could forget Tony the Mail Man! My wife wrote to me every day, and Tony made sure the mail went through. (All you readers out there with the mailman jokes, forget it!)

A few months before I left for Vietnam I had met Stan Bedard. (A Sailor Came to Newport) I still had my job cleaning the Moose Lodge each morning. Stan was in charge and urged me to join the Moose. I did and made some great friends. While away two very special members, Little Joe Silvia and Jiggs Daniels would frequently call to make sure my family was well.

My time in Newport was cut short. I got some bad news. The Navy was not going to let me stay in Newport but transfer me to the Naval Prison in Kittery, Maine.

After much discussion, it was decided that we would pack up and move to Kittery. We would rent our house in Newport while we were away. The relator taking charge of our property was Ray Swanner. (A Sailor came to Newport) Insurance was obtained from Roy Souza. (A sailor came to Newport)

Our arrival in downtown Kittery, Maine left us all wanting to turn around and head back to Newport. The base was rather small but dwarfed by one humongous structure that sat on the shores of Seavey Island.

Getting gas at the base service station, I asked the attendant about the prison.

Lifting the hood to check the oil he never lost a beat as he expounded on Seavey Island.

"The tidal shifts off the ocean force treacherous currents to pass by the east side of the island. The currents are so turbulent that in the history of the prison no inmate ever tried escaping by swimming the channel."

Closing the hood he wiped his hands on a rag.

"Your oil is good, whenever you ask about the prison refer to it as the "Castle." When it was first built, it was referred to as the Alcatraz of the east."

I figured he earned a two-dollar tip for sharing his information. The truth of the matter was that I never realized the Navy had a prison.

The first order of business was to find housing. It was available on the base however it had been built, in the early nineteen forty's. The housing office welcomed us to take a drive and look around. They were all single type buildings about the size of a log cabin. Each building had cement supports holding up the foundation but they were slowly sinking into the ground. The interior was small with two small bedrooms and an efficiency kitchen. Having three children it would be tight for them living in one room. Returning to the office we had no choice but to go for one of the units. The housing had been declared unsuitable meaning that we would only have to pay half of our housing allowance. I soon learned the Irony of living in condemned Navy housing, built in 1942, and the fairly new Air Force housing across the river. The housing office gave each of us four gallons of gloss blue to paint our unit. While at the Air force housing, they were having major problems trying to match their curtains with bedspreads.

Half ass settled in it was time for me to check in. I found a parking lot for staff parking. From there to the front gate was a short walk. The gate was in two parts. A large gate allowed vehicles through and a walkway gate for individual entry. As you passed through the gate, you held up your identification to a Marine guard. He in turn checks you out and gives you permission to enter.

My first impression inside the Castle was, "Holy Shit!"

The Medical Department was on the sixth floor. That became a major problem when the elevator crapped out. It was cement steps all the way. By the time you got to the sixth floor your knees were ready to buckle and your ass was dragging.

I just don't know how many single cells there was in a cellblock. I know it went five to six tiers high plus wrapping around with the same amount on the backside. All prisoners wore a gray like uniform with the large letters CMP imprinted across the rear end of the trousers. (Court Martial Prisoner)

CMP's residing in the cellblock were fed and lived in their cell. The only way out was take a job in one of the prison factories. With good conduct and a satisfactory work ethic, he would be moved from the cellblock to one of the four open dormitories.

The top row of cells was kept exclusively for homosexuals. That's a story within it self.

Chapter 39

I believe there are two types of personalities in this world. One enjoys and is fully content to work in a prison. The other wants no part of it. I am a member of that category. It's not a prison; it's a goddamn loony bin.

The medical department used prisoners for clerical work, keeping the area clean and assisting corpsmen with their work. These prisoners were mostly lifers. They do their time in Portsmouth until their entire military appeals come to an end. After that they are transferred to a penitentiary in their home state. If these poor bastards ever have a chance of freedom, their records had to reflect exceptional conduct. The rest of the population at the Castle was doing six months and a BCD (Bad Conduct Discharge) for doing some idiotic doodad crime listed in the Code of Military Justice. A large percentage was guilty of absent without leave. Disobeying orders, petty theft and smoking dope.

To put a prospective in my mind that made some sense to me. I always thought of it as six hundred Marines guarding six hundred Marines. The average CMP is not a fool. They can do six months time standing on their hands. Years ago a Bad Conduct Discharge meant you were condemned for life. Today people pay little significance or even care.

The truth of the matter was these prisoners do six months and go home. They have a full life ahead of them. Going back to Vietnam would mean putting one foot in the grave. On a daily basis CMP's made it a point to relate to the guards that soon they would be shipped back to Vietnam.

This constant discontentment among the guards and the prisoners resulted in the guards retaliating by pushing the rules to the limit.

The minute you step into a prison you have to accept that the guards are after the convicts and the convicts are after the guards. It goes on day after day. You can never be in the middle.

A CMP gave a guard a real mouth full of crap. Because of the rules the guard could not retaliate but merely put the CMP on report. Shuffling away, the CMP strutted his victory in front of his fellow inmates.

Submitting a request for a visitor takes three to four weeks. The visitor's center is located just outside the main gate.

On visitor's day, the CMP's would fall out in the prison yard for inspection then march to the visitor's center. The Guard in charge was well aware that the CMP who gave him a hard time was waiting in line to see his girlfriend. The duty sergeant slowly passed down the line stopping in front of the CMP.

"Excuse me CMP, but aren't you aware that shoes have to be shinned to enter the visitor's building?"

Right from the git go, the CMP knew he was about to be screwed over. It was payback time.

"Sergeant, my shoes are shinned, with your permission I would like to meet with my visitor."

The Sergeant waved one of his Corporals forward.

"Take these CMP's to the visitor's center, that is, all except this CMP with the dirty shoes. The CMP went ballistic to no avail. Four chasers appeared and quickly subdued him. (In order to be a chaser, you had to be at least six foot two inches and weigh in at two hundred ten pounds) The CMP wasn't giving up easily, he knew his girl friend was less than a hundred yards away, and these pricks were busting his balls. He got in a glancing blow off the top of Sergeant's head.

"Get the doc down here and throw this piece of shit in the hole."

The Chaser's dragged and pushed the CMP through a metal door that led to the area under the prison, well known as the dungeon. The cells were enclosed on all sides with the exception of a steel entrance door. Inside was a cast iron bed welded to the floor? In the lower corner was a circular hole rounded out

169

in the cement functioning as a toilet. There was no communication allowed. Every two days the hole would be flushed, the CMP removed from the cell, and given a three-minute shower. (Cold water)

A corpsman always present ensures that no brutality or harm is inflicted on a CMP. This was solitary confinement! Thirty days piss and punk. I have to admit I never went inside the cell and exited stage left when they took a CMP out of his cell. I had one hard fast rule. I see nothing, I know nothing, and I hear nothing.

I am a Navy Corpsman. Most of us have served with the Marines in combat. The prison is a Marine Command. I am very proud of being a "Doc" Marine. I have always received the deepest respect by the Marine Corps. If I reported a Marine guard for some infraction concerning a CMP, I might just as well commit Hari Kari.

Piss and Punk is the term for bread and water. In solitary, you would get half a loaf of bread and a quart of water. It was standard practice to pour the water into the half loaf of bread, open the cell door and throw it in.

A CMP went on a hunger strike and dropped about fifty pounds. He refused nourishment of any kind. His parents, a famous doctor and a group of supporters stood outside the prison gate demanding to see their son. The gates remain closed. When it was apparent that the CMP's life was in grave danger, it was told to me that the prison commander made him a visit. The conversation was some thing like this.

"Your life is in peril. Your parents and supporters are at the front gate demanding entry. I am here to tell you that's not going to happen. They won't see you until they take you out of here in a body bag. It's my choice, and I am going to let you die."

The CMP asked for nourishment.

One year to the day that I reported to the prison I requested that I be transferred to a ship in Newport. No problem, they sent me to a ship in Mayport, Florida.

Chapter 40

Disappointed at not being sent to Newport, we packed up and headed south. The ship was home ported at the U.S. Naval Station, Mayport, Florida.

With a large fleet of ships, including a couple of aircraft carriers home ported at Mayport the list for Naval Housing had no end.

We were fortunate in finding a house at Jacksonville Beach for rent. For the kids, it was great, as it was a five-minute walk to the beach. It was less than a twenty-minute ride to the base to shop at the Commissary or the Navy Exchange.

The ship was huge. It was a Second World War heavy cruiser that was converted in the yards at Boston, Massachusetts and leveled to the main deck. All the gun mounts were removed and replaced with new missile systems. There was a saying that barnacles never have the time to grow on the hull of a cruiser. Aboard less than two weeks and we got underway for the missile testing range somewhere in the vicinity of Puerto Rico. The crew numbered two thousand with the majority having something to do with the missile systems.

Everything was hush, hush! Top secret! What I had been able to surmise was that the ship carried two missile systems. Talos, which were long ranged and Tartar, short range. The missile storage areas were guarded twenty-four hours a day by a contingent of Marines. You could not enter those spaces without a proper clearance of secret.

When we got to the firing range, a Talos missile was to be launched off the fantail at an unmanned drone. A guess would be the drone was streaking across the blue sky going two to three hundred miles an hour. Against a perfect background, you could catch a glimpse of the drone. The Talos was fired, and all hands were watching as it ascended upward toward the drone. There was no escaping the Talos it hit the drone head-on. They both disintegrated on impact and what was left plummeted into the sea.

As I watched the destruction of the drone, I could not help but wonder why, if we had weapons like this, why in hell were we on the DMZ filling up body bags? Would it of been too much to ask of our government to deliver several Talos missiles on down town Hanoi and one right up Ho Chi Minh's ass? I mean they were the enemy. They were killing Marines. I drove my fellow ship mates loco for a couple of days and then put Vietnam to rest.

We steamed out of the Caribbean and into the Atlantic. The word was that we were going to Bermuda for the forth of July. Having nuclear warheads it made the ship the most powerful war ship in the world. Entering the harbor we were met by British officials. Having atomic weapons on board we were not allowed to enter their port.

So it was off to choice number two. We entered New York harbor and followed the Hudson River to a docking space a stone's throw away from New York City.

Several factions representing the city welcomed us. A representative from the USO handed out tickets for a Broadway show including lunch at the USO. They supplied transportation, so it was like a no-loose situation. Around thirty of us signed up.

The theater was rather small but comfortable. We had all taken our seats when the curtain opened as a parade of men and women pranced across the stage completely naked. The troops thought they had died and gone to heaven. The name of the play was, "Old Calcutta." We all agreed during lunch at the USO that it was one hell of a play. Several shipmates were trying to get tickets for the next performance.

Chapter 41

Life on board ship was pretty routine. It was a day in and day out existence. Work, eat and sleep. Not returning to Mayport, the ship steamed for the Mediterranean. Visiting various ports of call the local citizenry would look up at the Talos missiles in complete awe. They understood the concept of the missiles but had no way of comprehending the amount of destruction they could incur.

We returned to Mayport after being away for nine months, only to re-supply for a return trip back to the Mediterranean. Once again we were waving goodbye to our loved ones as the ship set a course to cross the Atlantic Ocean.

Sea stories are the life of a sailor's entertainment. Each story try's to out do the previous one. I'm going tell one of mine. We docked at the Rock of Gibraltar for three days of liberty and relaxation. You can well guess why it's called the rock. A short distance from the ship was a bar built into the stone. It was called the "Cave." When liberty call went, it didn't take the American Sailor long to find his way to that establishment.

Dimed lights with various naval ornaments hung above a long polished mahogany bar. A jukebox blared out spectacular rock and roll music echoing off the interior walls of the cave. What made this place spectacular was the fact that the booths lining the dance floor were overflowing with good-looking chicks.

There was no doubt, they had hit the mother lode. It didn't take a white hat long to strut his stuff over to one the booths and ask a young lady to dance. She refused, and to make matters worse they got up from the booths and began dancing with each other. Moving to the dance floor, the sailors tried to cut in to no avail. They asked the bar tender if the reason the girls wouldn't dance was because they were Americans? The bartender look perplexed.

175

"Nothing to do with it mates. You mention girls; there isn't a girl in the place. They're English Queens."

The cruise went uneventful. We visited several ports with all hands on good behavior and no earth shattering incidents. We were half way through the cruise and because of the budget being held up in Washington there was no oil to be had for the ship. We anchored in the bay of Athens, and the word was we could be there for several weeks.

Someone came up with the idea to charter a plane and fly back to Jacksonville. It sounded great. I was one of the first to come up with the ticket money. The plane was fully loaded when we took off from the Athens airport. A short time later the Captain announced a mechanical problem and that we would have to make a landing in Shannon, Ireland. We were informed that the repairs would take a couple of hours, and we would leave as soon as possible for Jacksonville.

Customs Agents met us as we debarked the plane. Because we had no passports we would be restricted to the inside of large building, and there would be customs agents stationed at each door. Lined up we semi marched from the runway to a large building a few hundred feet away. Once inside we found it to be the export building for Irish Whisky.

The repairs to the plane, took longer than expected. There was nothing to eat or drink in the building. No machines, no vendor's, just Irish whiskey. It was a happy crowd that landed in Jacksonville. Several needed assistance to get off the plane and there were at least two requiring stretchers.

All in all, we can always say we've been to Ireland. The trip back to Athens went much more smoothly. No Irish whiskey.

Once we were refueled our time was about up. Our relief ship arrived, and we were soon on our way back to Mayport.

It was a great arrival. My family came aboard to greet me. Although we were tied up to the pier, my wife got seasick.

I had completed my sea duty, and it was time to be transferred. I called the Bureau in Washington and explained to the detailer that we owned a home in Newport, and we so wanted to return there. He was polite but told me that there just weren't any billets open in Newport and that I might think of staying in Florida or Virginia.

It was a tough time for us. We notified our realtor that we would not be back and to sell the house. The sale was rather quick and in the same time frame the personnel office on the ship informed me that my orders were in.

"U.S. Naval Hospital, Newport, Rhode Island."

177

Chapter 42

It was extremely hard for all of us to leave Jacksonville and the Albany behind. The ship had a lot of away time in which shipmates aboard ship develop into one large family. The wives having the most difficult role of all; some how endured the long separations.

Forming a ship's wives association they bonded together in friend-ships that would last a lifetime. Our children had spent three years in the local school system and sadly said good-bye to their fellow students and favorite teachers. It was extremely hard for them, routine for a Navy family.

For me, it had been a great tour of duty. After the Marines, Vietnam and the Naval Prison the USS Albany was a great change of pace.

The Commanding Officer was Captain Robert G Peniston. (A sailor Came Newport) I would add, from having had Command of the Battleship, USS New Jersey.

The Executive Officer was Captain Richard Allen. (A sailor Came to Newport) They were the two most influential ranking officers that I ever had the privilege to know.

Under their leadership, the Albany was the pride of the sixth fleet. The only time I ever saw them riled was when the Albany docked in Northern Italy, and David E. took it upon himself to go on liberty!

I was proud to be in their Navy. You were clean-shaven, neat haircut, dress white uniform, bugle calls, ridged quarters, and a spotless ship all went to hell with the "Z" grams.

On arrival back to Mayport from a six month deployment, the ship was just approaching the breakwater when the word was passed for me to report to the bridge. That doesn't occur to often and on the way I was filled with mixed apprehensions.

"What did I do now?"

As I approached the open bridge the Executive Officer met me.

"The Captain requests that you stand by him on our arrival into port. If you ever served aboard ship you know there is no higher honor to be bestowed.

I looked down from the bridge at my wife and children standing on the pier, trying to find me at my usual deck formation. I could see the disappointment in my wife's face. It would never occur too her to look up to the bridge.

I kept waving fanatically each time she would look upward. Finely I was recognized and began waving in earnest. My wife's expression had changed to;

"What in hell is he doing up there?"

179

Chapter 43

Newport here we come again!! Household goods on their way we checked into the Naval Lodge. The shouts of joy coming across the Pell Bridge ensured that we were all very happy to return to our "home."

The Navy Lodge is a motel located out side of the base for active duty personnel to stay economically while seeking out permanent housing. Believe me, they are fully equipped.

The trip from Mayport had been uneventful with the exception of a stop in the nations capital. We had a new member of the family traveling with us. His name was Snoopy, and he was a big eared, short legged, Bassett Hound!

My aunt and uncle both worked in the nations capital. My aunt had worked in the Pentagon for more than thirty years and my uncle with the Defense Department for the same length of time.

They insisted that on our way to Newport that we stop and spend a day with them. My uncle made all the arrangements, and when we arrived, we were shocked at the size and grandeur of the hotel. I just knew that the welcome sign was not out for a Bassett hound.

My uncle had assured me that the hotel had a kennel for pets. Snoopy would not be a problem. I could tell that was not going to happen by the look on my approaching uncles face. There was no kennel!

After a heated discussion, the manager asked if it would be okay to put Mr. Snoopy in a storeroom in the basement, with a blanket, water and a cool room temperature. We all agreed and left Snoopy in the linen locker.

The hotel was most elegant. I spent most of my time having the kids show me all the amenities. The luxury of the hotel was a fascination to all of us.

Dressed for dinner, we all met in the main lobby. Talk about being overwhelmed the five of us stood with our mouths open. Uncle George had a grin cross his face as he waved for the hostess to escort us to our table.

Talk about first class, the waiter was wearing a tux! Scanning the room I was in awe. Men were attired in their military uniforms with medals concealing most of their upper body. Numerous patrons were dressed in long flowing robes wearing an assortment of various colored caps. My aunt explained that the colors of the various caps represented the country they were from. We couldn't help but stare at the men wearing large head turbans and their colorful silk waistbands.

In the center of the dinning room was a small, slow, revolving platform. It held thee musicians that were impeccably attired. A very graceful young lady bowed a fantastic looking violin; an elderly gentleman sat in the middle of the platform playing a very soft cello. He flanked by a second violin player as remarkable as the first.

They were playing a movement from Beethoven's 8th Symphony! No, I'm lying; this sailor didn't have a clue to what they were playing. What made it interesting is was the sound just above the music. It was sort of like the howl of a hound dog!

The expressions on the patrons faces showed that they heard it, not quite sure of it, and where in the hell was it coming from. The trio would play; the hound would howl. The trio stopped the howling stopped. The trio was visibly upset.

The hotel manager approached my Uncle and said they would make an exception and would we take the dog to our room. I was elected for that duty.

I brought Snoopy to the sixth floor showed him the room he promptly stretched out on a twin bed. When I shut the door to return to the dinning room, he was sound a sleep!

Chapter 44

The Navy Lodge gave us enough time to start our search for a place to live. We drove by our sold house in tears.

Directly across from Lodge was "Chicken City," the girls loved it. I swear they ate a ton of chicken wings.

As things settled down I would make a quick trip across the street to "La Fiesta," for a cold draft beer. The La Fiesta was located on the corner of Connell Highway and West Main Road. It was directly across the street from "Ann's Kitchen," another popular white hat water-ing hole.

The La Fiesta was your typical neighborhood joint. The owner catered to sailors and civilians alike; anyone with a dollar bill was welcomed. I would have a couple of glasses of beer and leave. I was never asked for an I.D.

While on the subject; there were two other establishments where I was served. The Lobster Claw on Bridge Street, the reason being the bar tender was a good friend. (A sailor came to Newport) The other bar was often so crowded that if you couldn't get served, some one would buy it for you. It was the "Driftwood," located on Connell Highway. There was a path behind it that led through a swamp to the naval hospital.

So much for sailors and their under age consumption. I must admit that I never was served in a bar along Thames Street. The exception was "McGee's." Nightly there were a thousand underage sailors all vying to find a bar on Thames Street that would serve them.

At a later date, I would meet Jerry Connell, who informed me that Connell Highway was named in the memory of his brother, a pilot who was killed in action during the Second World War.

With our house sold we were on the hunt for affordable housing. Driving back through Mahon Street in the Tomony Hill Housing Project was enough to know that radical changes took over since we left. Broken windows; litter throughout, and the sacred trash cans dented, dirty and in the street. What lawns we had were now dirt and mud. Would it be safe to live there?

People who have nothing to gain don't give a shit and Mahon Street proved it. Leaving the area, we all agreed that Mahon Street was out of the question. Sam Dawley must of retired or died!

Bill and Francis had both retired and at Colonial Realty we met up with Ray Swanyer. (A sailor came to Newport) A retired Chief he almost immediately showed us a three-story house off Rhode Island Avenue. It was big, empty, and affordable. We all went for it including Snoopy.

It was empty and our household goods were still parked on Inter-State 95. Making a trip to the base the Hospitably Center loaned us up with folding cots, blankets, pillows, pots, pans, silverware, coffee pot and a new tea kettle. We were almost Newporter's again. Couldn't declare that until we got our first tax bill. Our newly met neighbors Jim and Virginia Thurman were of enormous help; welcoming us and aiding us in making a new home. (A Sailor Came to Newport)

Our furniture arrived and we set about setting up shop. With thee floors every body had a room. Problem! The girls were scared to go up to the third floor. There were ghosts lurking about.

I took out the old gas fixtures, wallpapered and painted. The two rooms on the third floor came out real nice. Still they resisted. Then came the pajama party on the third floor. That night the partygoers' screaming was so loud they could have very well woke up a ghost.

The next morning the girls were camped out in the living room. Not a soul was on the third floor.

The cellar in this house was huge but more than that the furnace was humongous. When it lit off, I swear it sounded like it could get a destroyer underway. I hated to find out how many gallons the oil tank held.

When the oilman came I would have to have a sign saying, "DON'T FILL IT UP!"

Chapter 45

My leave came to an end, so it was time to report to the Naval Hospital for duty. For some reason, I felt somewhat anxious.

How long and how many paths had I traveled since I first walked up these steps. I walked pass the front desk and down the steps to the personnel office. I laid my orders on the exact counter I had placed my first set of orders. The Chief was gone, and so was Smithy. The faces would all be new. The next place I would go was the galley to see if any of my old friends were still there.

A Third Class Wave (A Sailor Came to Newport) was sitting behind Smithy desk with a tired and bored look about her. An expressionless face glanced up at me.

"Can I help you?"

I remembered the ass chewing I got the first time I arrived.

"Yes, you certainly may. You can begin by calling me by my first name!"

Startled she stood and came around her desk like I might be trying to come on to her.

"It's Chief; I don't mean to stand here and have my first name disregarded, which I might add is second only to God's, by a Third Class Petty Officer."

She blushed and moved away.

"You're about to give this Chief a check in list and directions. Then I am going to tell you I will be sitting at your desk while you run around and check me in."

It looked like she was becoming defiant; I could see she was going to resist. Before that could happen I cut her off?

"Now, if you insist on not doing what I asked, then here is food for thought. I'm here for a while. If we stand the duty watch together or if we work together or if you should get in some sort of difficulty I will be there to make your life miserable. Got it??"

"I got it CHIEF."

Grabbing up my check in sheet, she stormed out of the office. Watching her go her looks, and dark features reminded me of Judy J., who was a Wave in my class in Corps school.

She also had orders to the hospital. She was assigned to the X-ray Department. It wasn't long, and her, and the Chief Radiologist got caught doing the dirty deed in the Dark Room! It was a "hoot" in the Chief's mess.

To my displeasure I was assigned as Chief of the Maintenance Department. A truly boring and no action position. I felt like a civil service worker.

The Waves barracks had been torn down, and the interior of the corpsmen's quarters was soon to follow. Enlisted personnel were now housed on the main base and shuttled back and fourth.

Contracts had gone out to have several of the P-wards demolished. The Nurses quarters were closed and the building boarded up. It didn't a rocket scientist to know the hospital would be the next to go.

Chapter 46

The kids checked into the Newport School System and were very busy making friends. Meanwhile, my wife applied for a job at a local school for Teachers Aid and was accepted. Now I had a working wife.

I was standing night duty when I determined there were better things I could be doing. I called the garage and ordered the duty driver, (A Sailor came to Newport) to drive a car up to the main hospital.

Having to get dressed, break out a vehicle and do the paper work; he was notably pissed off when he arrived. Getting in the front seat beside him, I put my finger to my lips and pointed toward the gate and then down

Second Street. Turning onto Walnut Street, I had him pull to the curb and stop.

I got out, crossed the street and went into the package store. Bought a six-pack and got back in the car. The driver was looking some scared. This was some serious shit against the Code of Military Justice.

I motioned to return to the hospital. Going through the front gate, I directed him to drive down behind the old corpsmen's barracks.

Pulling into a dark empty parking space, I puled the tabs on one of the cans and handed it to him. He didn't hesitate for a moment and took it. This would be his sea story for many years to come. He was my kind of a sailor. Where was Francis when I fucking needed him?

Back in 59 he pulled this same stunt on me when he was on nights, and I was the duty driver. Damn it was wrong, and I could have been the subject to a court martial but after all this time! "Francis this is to you."

I told the E-3 the whole story. Now he had my sea story. We could have both been hanged at the yardarm. Stepping out of the car I threw the remaining four cans into the bay. I had pushed the system far enough.

The next morning I was at the Master Chiefs Office requesting an immediate transfer. I was nearing twenty years of service, and as I looked back on my career, I had done every thing expected of a corpsman but became a diver or go to sea on a destroyer as and Independent corpsman.

I wanted the experience of being at sea and having the medical responsibility of two hundred sailors under my care. I knew I could handle it.

The Master Chief smiled and wasted no time in getting me sent to a destroyer in Mayport! I would be at sea and with my enlistment running out, the family stayed in Newport.

It was just as well, As I boarded the ship I learned that the ship had been on a cruise to Northern Europe, and scuttlebutt was that it was slated for a yard overall. That would mean Philadelphia Naval Ship Yard.

The ship stood down along side the pier, giving the crew priority to reunite with their relatives and loved ones.

I learned my way around the ship and on the second day the First Class Corpsman that had been aboard left for duty in California. I was not too happy with the ship; it was dirty and housed a multitude of cockroaches. No sprayer or insecticide was aboard. It would be my first requisition.

A week or so had passed when the word was passed that a body was floating between the ship and the pier pilings. Taking a look see, it was evident it was a sailor dressed in dungarees, floating face down.

Finding the ships only body bag, I left the ship by the Quarter Deck, walked along the pier and lowed my self down on to the pilings. There were two pilings, side by side, approximately two feet across. Their main purpose was to keep the ship from rubbing up against the pier.

I had enough room to spread the body bag out and still be able to grab on the body. Looking up, the main deck was about fifteen feet above me. It was lined with the ships crew. I shouted up.

"Someone want to give me a hand?"

There were no volunteers. I knew what was coming. They didn't. Reaching over the body bag, I grabbed his shirt by the neck and the bottom of the pant leg.

With a quick jerking motion, I lifted him upward lying him with his back down on the body bag. His face was gruesome. The crabs had eaten about half of it, but the skin on his legs, arms and hands were pretty well intact. Looking back up to the deck, only the Executive Officer was there! The decks were deserted.

"I know who he is Doc, off this ship."

With that he turned and strode away leaving me to figure a way to get the body up on to the pier. It was simple. Wait for an ambulance and let them do it. Within ten minutes an ambulance arrived, and two corpsmen jumped down to help me. I liked being a Chief!

We left Mayport and steamed to Charleston, South Carolina, to off load ammunition. Completed we headed for the Philadelphia Naval Ship Yards. As I remember, it was the end of the year and got cold.

When we arrived the ship was lowered down on to a dry dock, water pumped out then the crew was sent to berth on a houseboat. It was tied up on the Delaware River. It sucked; it was cold, icy and miserable.

The houseboat was old; it stunk from the river water and was tied up to pilings in the middle of nowhere. I went home on weekends to survive. There was a Naval Hospital just out side the gate, and a large Dispensary located in the shipyard. Not much for me to do but give directions.

Traveling Amtrak, the train stopped in Providence, then I would catch a bus to Newport. Sunday night I caught the Midnight Special, Providence to Philadelphia. I had been around the world, but I never saw so many whores working a bus station like in Providence.

One night on the way, back the train stopped at the Old Seabrook Station. It was the usual stop. Several of us passengers were a sleep in the end car.

The absence of the trains "click clack" woke us up in complete darkness. The car wasn't moving. Looking out the windows, we could make out that we were sitting on a sidetrack. Evidently they thought the car was empty, unhooked and left.

A site it must have been to see ten or more people towing their bags and walking the tracks. Thankfully the station wasn't far but closed. We hit the stations outdoor benches and waited for the early morning crew. It was the only time I was listed as AWOL on the ships muster.

The Philadelphia Phillies baseball people were the best. We could watch all home games for fifty cents. The seats were bleaches but believe me we were thankful. Most of the crew became Philly fans.

Of course, we had to walk approximately a quarter of a mile to the stadium in groups of ten for personal safety.

Chapter 47

Finely, after several months we left the shipyard and steamed back the same route we had come. We arrived in Mayport to the scuttlebutt that the ship was slated to leave for a six-month cruise to the Mediterranean. That would put me over my enlistment. To go I would have to re-enlist?

Our schedule consisted of the ship going to sea each day and returning each night to finalize and shake down all the new improvements and additions.

The yard had installed a sewage-holding tank over the top of the fresh water holding tank!

"What about contamination?" You ask.

Simple! Have the corpsman check for leaks every eight hours. He merely wraps a paper towel around each fitting leading to the holding tank. Hold it for fifteen seconds, if dry moves on. If it detects moisture, he contacts the Chief Engineer!

He disliked corpsman immensely. He could never grasp the fact that the Geneva Convention restricted my duties; I could not stand watch or be directly involved in aiding the operation of a war ship.

For reason's unknown, I pissed this ring knocker off. I always made a point of smiling when I met him in the passageway. Once he stopped me and asked if I knew when I approached an officer it was customary to render a hand salute. I replied I would if I ever met one! That was it. We never spoke again. Damn I liked being a Chief!

I was given a sling psychrometer. It was a thing of beauty and underway I would go in the hole and stand in front of the evaporators. With a chart in one hand and the slinger in the other I could figure the length of time a Snipe (Engineering personnel) could stand a watch without any medical endangerments to his person. If the chart indicated the watch stander was in danger I would notify the Engineering Officer to relieve him. This was a definite medical problem. I always got one standard order.

"Find some dumb ass on this ship to relieve him, if not get the fuck out of my Engine Room!"

I could tell he liked me, and the program was working.

Some of the sailors on the ship were using various drugs at sea with no apparent problem. (Scuttlebutt) They had a million hiding places to keep their stash.

To combat this minute problem, each day I was to collect ten urine specimens from the crew. To guard against contamination, I was to personally carry them to the dispensary for testing. Two days later I would get the results.

Let's say I had three positives out of the ten. I would report this information to the Officer responsible for the program.

He would look the list over then hand it back.

"I know these three sailors very well Chief. They have to be false positives. Are you sure your bottles were sterile? Some how they got contaminated."

It went on day after day. Truth? They couldn't afford to loose any more crewmembers; they were operating with a skeleton crew as it was.

Chapter 48

The time passed quickly and before long I had to make a decision.

1. Ship over. The chances of being promoted to E8 was nil.
2. I would be going to port of calls that I had visited many times before.
3. I would ride the Atlantic testing the holding tanks and slinging my psychrometer.
4. Killing cockroaches, doing drug testing and treating the clap

I came to a decision!

Door number **5**

What more could I ask for? Been there, done that. I had a confirmed kill count of over two thousand cockroaches. This was a no-brainer. NEWPORT here I come.

Looking down from the Pell Bridge at one of one of the greatest harbors in the world I could not stop thinking back to 1958, when

(A **Sailor Came to Newport)** it was sailors, wine, women, and Jim McGrath singing, "Good Morning Captain."

Epilogue

Ode To A Sailor by Gene B. Trotta

(As written)

*I have a sailor boy with a heart so true,
Who looks like a million in his navy blue,
With his shoes spit-shined and his little white cap
He is sailing the seas all over the map.*

*He works from dawn until late at night,
Dispatching his duties with all his might.
It's "Yes Sir," "No Sir" and restrictions galore;
And if he doesn't obey them, there are more.*

*When he gets liberty and goes into port,
He and his buddies find the hours too short.
They head for the town, to take in the sights;
Alas, occasionally, they get into fights.*

*When he is alone, and it's time for "lights out,"
He aches with homesickness, of this*

there's no doubt.
He tries to remember all his parents have told him,
And worries, fearing that he might fail them.

He thinks of his mother, and the laughter they shared.
Of the talks that she gave him, so he'd be prepared;
He thinks of his family and friends left at home
When he joined the service, to go it--alone.

He is proud of his flag, ship, and uniform;
And is as neat as a pin, when it is worn.
He is proud of the stripes he wears on his sleeve,
And we are proud of him, this you can believe!

He has given up a lot, for you and me,
And for the Red, White, and Blue, of his Country!
When his hitch is up, and no more will roam,
We will welcome him back, to his beloved home.

The End

OTHERS NOVELS
BY
Edward T Duranty

NEWPORT

NEWPORT 2 THE RETURN OF
THERESA

WILFRED THE DEVIL'S
DISCIPLE

SAMUEL OWENS THE PIG BOY

ME - VITAMIN E –MOSES AND
LUCIFER

BILLY ONE EYE

www.edwardtduranty.com
www. Amazon.com
www. Barnes Nobel, Middletown, RI
Island Books, Middletown, RI

The Author (A Sailor Came to Newport)

Edward T Duranty is from the White Mountains of New Hampshire. Graduated from Whitefield School and enlisted in the U.S. Navy. He served aboard three ships, the Naval Hospital, Newport and as a Combat Corpsman with the 3rd Marine Division, Vietnam. He attended and received his BS degree at Salve Regina University. He is a member of the American Legion, Veterans of Foreign Wars and the Disabled American Veterans.

In appreciation

My Wife, Elaine

Sherry Duranty

Nancy Peterson

Kathy Crites